Edmund Burke

Two Speeches on Conciliation with America

And Two Letters on Irish Questions

Edmund Burke

Two Speeches on Conciliation with America
And Two Letters on Irish Questions

ISBN/EAN: 9783744687720

Printed in Europe, USA, Canada, Australia, Japan

Cover: Foto ©ninafisch / pixelio.de

More available books at **www.hansebooks.com**

𝕭𝖆𝖑𝖑𝖆𝖓𝖙𝖞𝖓𝖊 𝕻𝖗𝖊𝖘𝖘

BALLANTYNE, HANSON AND CO., EDINBURGH
CHANDOS STREET, LONDON

TWO SPEECHES

ON

CONCILIATION WITH AMERICA

AND

TWO LETTERS ON IRISH QUESTIONS

BY

EDMUND BURKE

WITH AN INTRODUCTION BY HENRY MORLEY

LL.D., PROFESSOR OF ENGLISH LITERATURE AT
UNIVERSITY COLLEGE, LONDON

LONDON

GEORGE ROUTLEDGE AND SONS

BROADWAY, LUDGATE HILL

NEW YORK: 9 LAFAYETTE PLACE

1886

INTRODUCTION.

In July 1765 Edmund Burke, then thirty-five years old, began his
political career as secretary to the Marquis of Rockingham, who had
just undertaken the formation of a Ministry. Burke presently entered
Parliament as member for Wendover, through the interest of Lord
Verney. The American colonies were at that time united in vigorous
resistance to a Stamp Act, which involved claim and use of the right of
an English Parliament to impose direct taxes on colonies that were not
represented in it.

There had been indirect taxation since the days of our English
Commonwealth, when the Navigation Act of 1651 required all colonial
exports to England to be shipped only in American or English vessels.
After the Restoration, a second Navigation Act, in 1660, ordered that
most of the exports from the colonies should be shipped only to England
or to an English colony, and in American or English vessels. In 1663
a third Navigation Act required that most of the imports into the colonies
should be shipped only from England or an English colony, and in
American or English vessels. In 1672 there were added duties upon
certain enumerated articles, in passing from one colony to another. This
involved the establishment of royal custom-houses and revenue officers
in service of the Crown. In Massachusetts these changes were opposed;
the General Court of the colony resolved "that the Acts of Navigation are
an invasion of the rights and privileges of the subjects of his Majesty in
this colony, they not being represented in the Parliament." In 1680
a notice of the appointment of a collector of the royal customs for New
England was torn down at Boston by order of the colonial magistrates.
The opposition was not effectual, and the number of revenue officers
increased.

In 1696 a Board of Trade was established, consisting of a President
and seven members, entitled the Lords Commissioners for Trade and
Plantations. Among other duties this body had charge of the execution of the Navigation Acts, and it was to bring the colonies more
strictly under royal control. The Board of Trade proposed, therefore, in 1697, the appointment of a captain-general, with absolute
power to levy and organize an army without reference to any colonial

authority. In 1698 it prohibited the export of colonial woollens even from one colony to another. In 1706 it recommended, but did not obtain, the resumption of charters still held by some of the colonies. In 1714 a Secretary of State was made chief of the Board of Trade. The Duke of Newcastle, who held this office from 1724 to 1748, supposed New England to be an island.

The operations of the Royal African Company, which had been first formed in 1618, reconstituted in 1631, and again in 1663, and which acquired wealth by the trade in slaves, were at the same time promoted. The Treaty of Utrecht, in 1713, contained a contract on the part of Spain that Great Britain alone should supply her colonies with slaves; and in 1750 Great Britain received, by the Treaty of Aix-la-Chapelle, an indemnity of a hundred thousand pounds for giving up this right. When Virginia and South Carolina laid a prohibitory duty on the importation of slaves, their acts were annulled by royal command. In 1750, when the trade in slaves was made independent of this company, the reason given in the British Parliament was that "the slave trade is very advantageous to Great Britain." The colonists of the Southern States of America had therefore endeavoured in vain to check the importation of slave labour.

In 1733 the Molasses Act laid duties in the American colonies upon molasses, sugar, and rum imported from any but the British West India Islands. The agent of New York in England protested that this was "divesting the colonists of their rights as the king's natural-born subjects and Englishmen, in levying subsidies upon them against their own consent." In 1732 the American colonists were forbidden to export hats; in 1750 they were forbidden to erect mills for slitting or rolling iron, or furnaces for making steel.

In 1754 the Mutiny Act, providing for the discipline and quarters of the English army, was extended to the colonies. In 1755 the Earl of Loudoun was sent over as Governor of Virginia, and commander-in-chief over the thirteen colonies of America. Permanence of the appointment of judges was next struck at; their commissions were issued, which were to run no longer "during good behaviour," but "during the king's pleasure." New York in 1761 refused to pay the salary of a chief justice appointed, and he procured for himself from the Board of Trade a grant to be paid from the quit-rents of the province. There came claims also in 1761 for writs of assistance authorizing search for goods imported in defiance of the acts of trade.

Thus a long course of unwise policy had raised a spirit of antagonism, and much advance had been made towards the alienation of the American colonies, when there was added for the first time a direct taxatoin for revenue to the long series of taxations for regulation of trade. At the beginning of the year 1764 the British Parliament voted that it had a right to tax the colonies. George Grenville by the Sugar Act in 1764 laid duties upon sugar and other articles of colonial import. By the Stamp Act in 1765 he imposed in the American colonies a stamp duty, like that in England, upon business documents and newspapers.

This disregard of American feeling not only gave new force to the growing discontent, but provoked the organizing of resistance. Massachusetts proposed a Colonial Congress at New York, which first met on the 7th of October 1765, and twelve days afterwards, on the 19th of October, agreed to a Declaration of Rights.

Just in this critical time the Ministry of Lord Rockingham had newly taken the responsibility of government. Lord Rockingham—himself no speaker; one who had been attacking him was asked, "How could you worry a poor, dumb creature so?"—made Burke his private secretary, brought Burke into the House of Commons, and spoke through the voice of Burke. If Burke did not inspire his American policy, the policy was also Burke's, and Burke was its great interpreter. The Ministry was Whig ; but Burke was essentially Conservative. He had the practical mind of a statesman ; and he strongly dreaded revolutionary change. Inconsiderate zeal to force the colonies into submission to imperial claims, against which opposition was fast rising to revolutionary heat, he met by steady labour in the interests of peace. The Stamp Act was repealed, and Parliament satisfied itself with the assertion of imperial right to tax. Assert by all means, argued Burke, your right to tax the colonies directly for imperial revenue. If you take care never to exercise the right, it will be undisputed. Be taught by the experience that shows the peril of enforcing such a right. The Rockingham Ministry was followed in July 1766 by that of the elder Pitt, who took only a small office in his own Ministry, and with it a peerage as Earl of Chatham. The Duke of Grafton took the place at the head of the Treasury vacated by Lord Rockingham, and the Ministry included men who would be foremost in enforcing rights of taxation against the colonists.

American opposition was disarmed by the repeal of the Stamp Act ; statues were voted to Pitt and to the king ; removal of the active cause of irritation brought back the old spirit of loyalty ; while at home the Parliament of 1767 was reversing all the policy of peace. I created a Board of Revenue Commissioners for America ; it passed a Tea Act that imposed duties on tea and other imports into the colonies. as means of providing for payment of troops and for the salaries of royal governors and judges ; it also declared the New York Assembly incapable of legislation until it had assented to the Quartering Act of 1765. In 1768 the ordering of British troops into Boston, to control the public feeling excited by this policy of coercion, led to the gathering of a convention from all Massachusetts, that urged in vain upon the governor the summoning of the Legislature. In 1769 a new Act of Parliament directed that all cases of treason in the colonies should be tried in the mother country. This drew from Washington the declaration that no man should scruple or hesitate a moment to use arms in defence of freedom. "Yet arms, I would beg leave to add, should be the last resource."

In 1770 the Assembly of Virginia endeavoured to lay restrictions on the slave trade ; but the royal Governor was at once directed by the Ministry at home to consent to no laws affecting the interests of the slave-dealers. Attempts of other colonies in the same direction were met in the same way. By 1773 the irritation of the colonists had been urged so far that three ships in the port of Boston, bringing cargoes of tea upon which duty was to be raised, were boarded and their tea thrown into the dock.

The Duke of Grafton's Ministry had been succeeded by that of Lord North who ruled as agent for the king, and during the whole of his disastrous Ministry, from 1770 to 1782, the country suffered from that interference of the king and the king's friends which Burke condemned in 1773 in his *Thoughts on the Cause of the Present Discontents*. It was on the 19th of April 1774 that Burke made the famous speech on *American Taxation* which is the first piece in the present volume.

In 1774, at a meeting of the county of Fairfax, with George Washington in the chair, it was resolved " that during our present difficulties and distress no slaves ought to be imported into any of the British colonies on this continent; and we take this opportunity of declaring our most earnest wishes to see an entire stop for ever put to such a wicked, cruel, and unnatural trade.

The Government at home met opposition by enactments that virtually deprived Massachusetts of its charter, and placed it under strict British rule. Virginia voted in May 1774 that an attack upon one colony was an attack upon all British America, and recommended a General Congress, which first met as the Continental Congress at Philadelphia on the 5th of September 1774. On the 20th of October it signed the agreement that established the American Association. On the day of the separation of this Congress, October 26th, the Congress of Massachusetts organized its militia, and began to prepare for the alternative of forcible resistance. Other colonies followed the example.

In the month of the first meeting of the Continental Congress at Philadelphia there was a general election in England, swayed by strong feeling against the colonists, and a large majority was returned of members pledged to a policy of coercion. Burke entered that Parliament as member for Bristol, then the second town in the kingdom; and on the 22nd of March 1775 he laid before the House of Commons thirteen resolutions for reconcilement with America, and made the greatest of all his speeches, that on *Conciliation with America*, which is also contained in this volume. The resolutions were rejected by a vote on the first of 270 against 78.

On the 19th of April 1775 occurred, at Lexington and Concord, the first serious affray between British soldiers and colonial militia. The British were repulsed, and about three hundred were killed, wounded, or taken prisoners.

On the 10th of May a new Congress assembled in Philadelphia; and on the 15th of June George Washington received his commission as Commander-in-Chief of the Army of the United Colonies. Until after the rejection of a second petition of Congress in 1775, " I never," said John Jay, " heard an American of any class or of any description express a wish for the independence of the colonies." But the wish now was forced upon the colonists, and a Declaration of American Independence, having obtained the unanimous vote of all the colonies, was adopted on the 4th of July 1776. Finally, after a vain struggle, into which the mother country was misled, American Independence was obtained by treaties signed with the United States on the 3rd of September 1783.

H. M.

May 1866.

Burke's Two Speeches

CONCILIATION WITH AMERICA.

—◦◦◦—

AMERICAN TAXATION.

Sir,—I agree with the honourable gentleman who spoke last, that this subject is not new in this House. Very disagreeably to this House, very unfortunately to this nation, and to the peace and prosperity of this whole empire, no topic has been more familiar to us. For nine long years, session after session, we have been lashed round and round this miserable circle of occasional arguments and temporary expedients. I am sure our heads must turn, and our stomachs nauseate with them. We have had them in every shape; we have looked at them in every point of view. Invention is exhausted; reason is fatigued; experience has given judgment; but obstinacy is not yet conquered.

The honourable gentleman has made one endeavour more to diversify the form of this disgusting argument. He has thrown out a speech

composed almost entirely of challenges. Challenges
are serious things ; and as he is a man of prudence
as well as resolution, I daresay he has very well
weighed those challenges before he delivered them.
I had long the happiness to sit at the same side of
the House, and to agree with the honourable gentleman on all the American questions. My sentiments,
I am sure, are well known to him ; and I thought I
had been perfectly acquainted with his. Though I
find myself mistaken, he will still permit me to use
the privilege of an old friendship ; he will permit me
to apply myself to the House under the sanction of
his authority ; and, on the various grounds he has
measured out, to submit to you the poor opinions
which I have formed upon a matter of importance
enough to demand the fullest consideration I could
bestow upon it.

He has stated to the House two grounds of
deliberation : one narrow and simple, and merely
confined to the question on your paper ; the other
more large and more complicated ; comprehending
the whole series of the parliamentary proceedings
with regard to America, their causes, and their consequences. With regard to the latter ground, he
states it as useless, and thinks it may be even dangerous, to enter into so extensive a field of inquiry.
Yet, to my surprise, he had hardly laid down this
restrictive proposition, to which his authority would
have given so much weight, when directly, and with

the same authority, he condemns it; and declares it
absolutely necessary to enter into the most ample
historical detail.   His zeal has thrown him a little
out of his usual accuracy.   In this perplexity what
shall we do, Sir, who are willing to submit to the law
he gives us?   He has reprobated in one part of his
speech the rule he had laid down for debate in the
other; and, after narrowing the ground for all those
who are to speak after him, he takes an excursion
himself, as unbounded as the subject and the extent
of his great abilities.

Sir, when I cannot obey all his laws, I will do the
best I can.   I will endeavour to obey such of them
as have the sanction of his example; and to stick to
that rule, which, though not consistent with the
other, is the most rational.   He was certainly in the
right when he took the matter largely.   I cannot
prevail on myself to agree with him in his censure
of his own conduct.   It is not, he will give me leave
to say, either useless or dangerous.   He asserts that
retrospect is not wise; and the proper, the only
proper, subject of inquiry, is "not how we got into
this difficulty, but how we are to get out of it."   In
other words, we are, according to him, to consult our
invention and to reject our experience.   The mode
of deliberation he recommends is diametrically opposite to every rule of reason and every principle of
good sense established amongst mankind.   For that
sense and that reason I have always understood

absolutely to prescribe, whenever we are involved in
difficulties from the measures we have pursued, that
we should take a strict review of those measures, in
order to correct our errors, if they should be corri-
gible ; or at least to avoid a dull uniformity in mischief, and the unpitied calamity of being repeatedly
caught in the same snare.

Sir, I will freely follow the honourable gentleman
in his historical discussion, without the least management for men or measures, further than as they shall
seem to me to deserve it.   But before I go into that
large consideration, because I would omit nothing
that can give the House satisfaction, I wish to tread
the narrow ground to which alone the honourable
gentleman, in one part of his speech, has so strictly
confined us.

He desires to know, whether, if we were to repeal
this tax, agreeably to the proposition of the honourable gentleman who made the motion, the Americans
would not take post on this concession, in order to
make a new attack on the next body of taxes ; and
whether they would not call for a repeal of the duty
on wine as loudly as they do now for the repeal of
the duty on tea ?   Sir, I can give no security on this
subject.   But I will do all that I can, and all that
can be fairly demanded.   To the experience which
the honourable gentleman reprobates in one instant,
and reverts to in the next ; to that experience, without the least wavering or hesitation on my part, I

steadily appeal; and would to God there was no other arbiter to decide on the vote with which the House is to conclude this day !

When Parliament repealed the Stamp Act in the year 1766, I affirm, first, that the Americans did not in consequence of this measure call upon you to give up the former parliamentary revenue which subsisted in that country, or even any one of the articles which compose it. I affirm also, that when, departing from the maxims of that repeal, you revived the scheme of taxation, and thereby filled the minds of the colonists with new jealousy and all sorts of apprehensions, then it was that they quarrelled with the old taxes, as well as the new ; then it was, and not till then, that they questioned all the parts of your legislative power; and by the battery of such questions have shaken the solid structure of this empire to its deepest foundations.

Of those two propositions I shall, before I have done, give such convincing, such damning proof, that however the contrary may be whispered in circles, or bawled in newspapers, they never more will dare to raise their voices in this House. I speak with great confidence. I have reason for it. The Ministers are with me. They at least are convinced that the repeal of the Stamp Act had not, and that no repeal can have, the consequences which the honourable gentleman who defends their measures is so much alarmed at. To their conduct I refer him for a con-

clusive answer to his objection. I carry my proof
irresistibly into the very body of both Ministry and
Parliament ; not on any general reasoning growing
out of collateral matter, but on the conduct of the
honourable gentleman's ministerial friends on the
new revenue itself.

The Act of 1767, which grants this tea duty, sets
forth in its preamble that it was expedient to raise a
revenue in America, for the support of the civil
government there, as well as for purposes still more
extensive. To this support the Act assigns six
branches of duties. About two years after this Act
passed, the Ministry—I mean the present Ministry—
thought it expedient to repeal five of the duties, and
to leave (for reasons best known to themselves) only
the sixth standing. Suppose any person, at the time
of that repeal, had thus addressed the Minister :
" Condemning, as you do, the repeal of the Stamp Act,
why do you venture to repeal the duties upon glass,
paper, and painters' colours ? Let your pretence for
the repeal be what it will, are you not thoroughly
convinced that your concessions will produce, not
satisfaction, but insolence, in the Americans ; and
that the giving up these taxes will necessitate the
giving up of all the rest ?" This objection was as
palpable then as it is now ; and it was as good for
preserving the five duties as for retaining the sixth.
Besides, the Minister will recollect that the repeal of
the Stamp Act had but just preceded his repeal ; and

the ill policy of that measure (had it been so impolitic as it has been represented), and the mischiefs it produced, were quite recent. Upon the principles therefore of the honourable gentleman, upon the principles of the Minister himself, the Minister has nothing at all to answer. He stands condemned by himself, and by all his associates, old and new, as a destroyer, in the first trust of finance, of the revenues ; and in the first rank of honour, as a betrayer of the dignity of his country.

Most men, especially great men, do not always know their well-wishers. I come to rescue that noble lord out of the hands of those he calls his friends, and even out of his own. I will do him the justice he is denied at home. He has not been this wicked or imprudent man. He knew that a repeal had no tendency to produce the mischiefs which give so much alarm to his honourable friend. His work was not bad in its principle, but imperfect in its execution ; and the motion on your paper presses him only to complete a proper plan, which, by some unfortunate and unaccountable error, he had left unfinished.

I hope, Sir, the honourable gentleman who spoke last, is thoroughly satisfied, and satisfied out of the proceedings of Ministry on their own favourite Act, that his fears from a repeal are groundless. If he is not, I leave him, and the noble lord who sits by him, to settle the matter, as well as they can,

together ; for if the repeal of American taxes destroys
all our government in America—he is the man !—
and he is the worst of all the repealers, because he is
the last.

But I hear it rung continually in my ears, now and
formerly—" The preamble ! what will become of the
preamble, if you repeal this tax ?"   I am sorry to be
compelled so often to expose the calamities and disgraces of Parliament.   The preamble of this law,
standing as it now stands, has the lie direct given to
it by the provisionary part of the Act; if that can be
called provisionary which makes no provision.   I
should be afraid to express myself in this manner,
especially in the face of such a formidable array of
ability as is now drawn up before me, composed of
the ancient household troops of that side of the
House, and the new recruits from this, if the matter
were not clear and indisputable.   Nothing but truth
could give me this firmness ; but plain truth and
clear evidence can be beat down by no ability.   The
clerk will be so good as to turn to the Act, and
to read this favourite preamble :

> Whereas it is expedient that a revenue should
> be raised in your Majesty's dominions in
> America for making a more certain and
> adequate provision for defraying the charge of
> the administration of justice, and support of
> civil government, in such provinces where it
> shall be found necessary ; and towards further

defraying the expenses of defending, protecting, and securing the said dominions.

You have heard this pompous performance. Now, where is the revenue which is to do all these mighty things? Five-sixths repealed—abandoned—sunk —gone—lost for ever. Does the poor solitary tea duty support the purposes of this preamble? Is not the supply there stated as effectually abandoned as if the tea duty had perished in the general wreck? Here, Mr. Speaker, is a precious mockery—a preamble without an Act—taxes granted in order to be repealed—and the reasons of the grant still carefully kept up! This is raising a revenue in America! This is preserving dignity in England! If you repeal this tax in compliance with the motion, I readily admit that you lose this fair preamble. Estimate your loss in it. The object of the Act is gone already; and all you suffer is the purging the Statute-book of the opprobrium of an empty, absurd, and false recital.

It has been said again and again, that the five taxes were repealed on commercial principles. It is so said in the paper in my hand; a paper which I constantly carry about; which I have often used, and shall often use again. What is got by this paltry pretence of commercial principles I know not: for if your government in America is destroyed by the repeal of taxes, it is of no consequence upon

what ideas the repeal is grounded.   Repeal this tax,
too, upon commercial principles if you please.   These
principles will serve as well now as they did formerly.
But your know that, either your objection to a repeal
from these supposed consequences has no validity,
or that this pretence never could remove it.   This
commercial motive never was believed by any man,
either in America, which this letter is meant to
soothe, or in England, which it is meant to deceive.
It was impossible it should.   Because every man, in
the least acquainted with the detail of commerce,
must know that several of the articles on which the
tax was repealed, were fitter objects of duties than
almost any other articles- that could possibly be
chosen ; without comparison more so, than the tea
that was left taxed ; as infinitely less liable to be
eluded by contraband.   The tax upon red and
white lead was of this nature.   You have, in this
kingdom, an advantage in lead, that amounts to a
monopoly.   When you find yourself in this situation
of advantage, you sometimes venture to tax even
your own export.   You did so soon after the last
war ; when, upon this principle, you ventured to
impose a duty on coals.   In all the articles of
American contraband trade, who ever heard of the
smuggling of red lead and white lead ?   You might
therefore, well enough, without danger of contraband
and without injury to commerce (if this were the
whole consideration), have taxed these commodities.

The same may be said of glass. Besides, some of the things taxed were so trivial, that the loss of the objects themselves, and their utter annihilation out of American commerce, would have been comparatively as nothing. But is the article of tea such an object in the trade of England as not to be felt, or felt but slightly, like white lead and red lead, and painters' colours? Tea is, an object of far other importance. Tea is perhaps the most important object, taking it with its necessary connections, of any in the mighty circle of our commerce. If commercial principles had been the true motives to the repeal, or had they been at all attended to, tea would have been the last article we should have left taxed for a subject of controversy.

Sir, it is not a pleasant consideration ; but nothing in the world can read so awful and so instructive a lesson as the conduct of Ministry in this business, upon the mischief of not having large and liberal ideas in the management of great affairs. Never have the servants of the State looked at the whole of your complicated interests in one connected view. They have taken things by bits and scraps, some at one time and one pretence, and some at another, just as they pressed, without any sort of regard to their relations or dependencies. They never had any kind of system, right or wrong ; but only invented occasionally some miserable tale for the day, in order meanly to sneak out of difficulties into which they

had proudly strutted. And they were put to all
these shifts and devices, full of meanness and full of
mischief, in order to pilfer piecemeal a repeal of an
Act which they had not the generous courage, when
they found and felt their error, honourably and
fairly to disclaim. By such management, by the
irresistible operation of feeble counsels, so paltry a
sum as threepence in the eyes of a financier, so
insignificant an article as tea in the eyes of a
philosopher, have shaken the pillars of a commercial
empire that circled the whole globe.

Do you forget that, in the very last year, you
stood on the precipice of general bankruptcy? Your
danger was indeed great. You were distressed in
the affairs of the East India Company; and you
well know what sort of things are involved in the
comprehensive energy of that significant appellation.
I am not called upon to enlarge to you on that
danger, which you thought proper yourselves to
aggravate, and to display to the world with all the
parade of indiscreet declamation. The monopoly of
the most lucrative trades, and the possession of
imperial revenues, had brought you to the verge of
beggary and ruin. Such was your representation—
such, in some measure, was your case. The vent of
ten millions of pounds of this commodity, now locked
up by the operation of an injudicious tax, and rotting
in the warehouses of the Company, would have prevented all this distress, and all that series of

desperate measures which you thought yourselves
obliged to take in consequence of it. America
would have furnished that vent, which no other part
of the world can furnish but America ; where tea is
next to a necessary of life, and where the demand
grows upon the supply. I hope our dear-bought
East India Committees have done us at least so
much good as to let us know that, without a more
extensive sale of that article, our East India
revenues and acquisitions can have no certain connection with this country. It is through the
American trade of tea that your East India conquests are to be prevented from crushing you with
their burthen. They are ponderous indeed ; and
they must have that great country to lean upon, or
they tumble upon your head. It is the same folly
that has lost you at once the benefit of the West
and of the East. This folly has thrown open fold-
ing-doors to contraband ; and will be the means of
giving the profits of the trade of your colonies to
every nation but yourselves. Never did a people
suffer so much for the empty words of a preamble.
It must be given up. For on what principles does
it stand ? This famous revenue stands, at this hour,
on all the debate, as a description of revenue not as
yet known in all the comprehensive (but too comprehensive !) vocabulary of finance—a preambulary
tax. It is indeed a tax of sophistry, a tax of
pedantry, a tax of disputation, a tax of war and

rebellion, a tax for anything but benefit to the imposers, or satisfaction to the subject.

Well! but whatever it is, gentlemen will force the colonists to take the teas. You will force them? Has seven years' struggle yet been able to force them? Oh, but it seems, " we are in the right. The tax is trifling—in fact, it is rather an exoneration than an imposition ; three-fourths of the duty formerly payable on teas exported to America is taken off; the place of collection is only shifted ; instead of the retention of a shilling from the draw-back here, it is threepence custom paid in America." All this, Sir, is very true. But this is the very folly and mischief of the Act. Incredible as it may seem, you know that you have deliberately thrown away a large duty which you held secure and quiet in your hands, for the vain hope of getting one three-fourths less, through every hazard, through certain litigation, and possibly through war.

The manner of proceeding in the duties on paper and glass, imposed by the same Act, was exactly in the same spirit. There are heavy excises on those articles when used in England. On export, these excises are drawn back. But instead of with-holding the drawback, which might have been done with ease, without charge, without possibility of smuggling, and instead of applying the money (money already in your hands) according to your pleasure, you began your operations in finance by

flinging away your revenue; you allowed the whole
drawback on export, and then you charged the duty
(which you had before discharged) payable in the
colonies, where it was certain the collection would
devour it to the bone, if any revenue were ever
suffered to be collected at all. One spirit pervades
and animates the whole mass.

Could anything be a subject of more just alarm
to America than to see you go out of the plain
high road of finance, and give up your most certain
revenues and your clearest interests, merely for the
sake of insulting your colonies? No man ever
doubted that the commodity of tea could bear an
imposition of threepence. But no commodity will
bear threepence, or will bear a penny, when the
general feelings of men are irritated, and two
millions of people are resolved not to pay. The
feelings of the colonies were formerly the feelings
of Great Britain. Theirs were formerly the feelings
of Mr. Hampden when called upon for the payment
of twenty shillings. Would twenty shillings have
ruined Mr. Hampden's fortune? No! but the
payment of half twenty shillings, on the principle
it was demanded, would have made him a slave.
It is the weight of that preamble, of which you
are so fond, and not the weight of the duty, that
the Americans are unable and unwilling to bear.

It is then, Sir, upon the principle of this measure,
and nothing else, that we are at issue. It is a

principle of political expediency. Your Act of
1767 asserts that it is expedient to raise a revenue
in America ; your Act of 1769, which takes away
that revenue, contradicts the Act of 1767 ; and, by
something much stronger than words, asserts that
it is not expedient. It is a reflection upon your
wisdom to persist in a solemn parliamentary declaration of the expediency of any object, for which,
at the same time, you make no sort of provision.
And pray, Sir, let not this circumstance escape you;
it is very material that the preamble of this Act,
which we wish to repeal, is not declaratory of a
right, as some gentlemen seem to argue it; it is
only a recital of the expediency of a certain exercise
of a right supposed already to have been asserted ;
an exercise you are now contending for by ways
and means which you confess, though they were
obeyed, to be utterly insufficient for their purpose.
You are therefore at this moment in the awkward
situation of fighting for a phantom, a quiddity, a
thing that wants, not only a substance, but even a
name ; for a thing which is neither abstract right
nor profitable enjoyment.

They tell you, Sir, that your dignity is tied to
it. I know not how it happens, but this dignity
of yours is a terrible incumbrance to you ; for it
has of late been ever at war with your interest,
your equity, and every idea of your policy. Show
the thing you contend for to be reason ; show it

to be common sense ; show it to be the means of
attaining some useful end ; and then I am content
to allow it what dignity you please. But what
dignity is derived from the perseverance in absurdity
is more than ever I could discern. The honourable
gentleman has said well—indeed, in most of his
general observations I agree with him—he says,
that this subject does not stand as it did formerly.
Oh, certainly not ! Every hour you continue on
this ill-chosen ground your difficulties thicken on
you ; and therefore my conclusion is, remove from
a bad position as quickly as you can. The disgrace,
and the necessity of yielding, both of them grow
upon you every hour of your delay.

But will you repeal the Act, says the honourable
gentleman, at this instant, when America is in open
resistance to your authority, and that you have just
revived your system of taxation ? He thinks he has
driven us into a corner. But thus pent up I am
content to meet him ; because I enter the lists
supported by my old authority, his new friends,
the Ministers themselves. The honourable gentleman remembers that, about five years ago, as great
disturbances as the present prevailed in America
on account of the new taxes. The Ministers represented these disturbances as treasonable ; and this
House thought proper, on that representation, to
make a famous address for a revival, and for a new
application of a statute of Henry the Eighth. We

besought the king, in that well-considered address, to inquire into treasons, and to bring the supposed traitors from America to Great Britain for trial. His Majesty was pleased graciously to promise a compliance with our request. All the attempts from this side of the House to resist these violences, and to bring about a repeal, were treated with the utmost scorn. An apprehension of the very consequences now stated by the honourable gentleman was then given as a reason for shutting the door against all hope of such an alteration. And so strong was the spirit for supporting the new taxes that the session concluded with the following remarkable declaration. After stating the vigorous measures which had been pursued, the Speech from the Throne proceeds :—

"You have assured me of your firm support in the prosecution of them. Nothing, in my opinion, could be more likely to enable the well-disposed among my subjects in that part of the world effectually to discourage and defeat the designs of the factious and seditious than the hearty concurrence of every branch of the Legislature in maintaining the execution of the laws in every part of my dominions."

After this no man dreamt that a repeal under this Ministry could possibly take place. The honourable gentleman knows, as well as I, that the idea was utterly exploded by those who sway the House.

This speech was made on the ninth day of May, 1769. Five days after this speech—that is, on the 13th of the same month, the public circular letter, a part of which I am going to read to you, was written by Lord Hillsborough, Secretary of State for the Colonies. After reciting the substance of the King's Speech, he goes on thus :—

"I can take upon me to assure you, notwithstanding insinuations to the contrary from men with factious and seditious views, that his Majesty's present Administration have at no time entertained a design to propose to Parliament to lay any further taxes upon America for the purpose of raising a revenue ; and that it is at present their intention to propose, the next session of Parliament, to take off the duties upon glass, paper and colours, upon consideration of such duties having been laid contrary to the true principles of commerce.

"These have always been, and still are, the sentiments of his Majesty's present servants, and by which their conduct in respect to America has been governed. And his Majesty relies upon your prudence and fidelity for such an explanation of his measures as may tend to remove the prejudices which have been excited by the misrepresentations of those who are enemies to the peace and prosperity of Great Britain and her colonies, and to re-establish that mutual confidence and affection upon which the glory and safety of the British empire depend."

Here, Sir, is a canonical book of ministerial scripture; the general epistle to the Americans. What does the gentleman say to it? Here a repeal is promised; promised without condition, and while your authority was actually resisted. I pass by the public promise of a peer relative to the repeal of taxes by this House. I pass by the use of the king's name in a matter of supply, that sacred and reserved right of the Commons. I conceal the ridiculous figure of Parliament, hurling its thunders at the gigantic rebellion of America; and then, five days after, prostrate at the feet of those assemblies we affected to despise, begging them, by the intervention of our ministerial sureties, to receive our submission, and heartily promising amendment. These might have been serious matters formerly; but we are grown wiser than our fathers. Passing, therefore, from the constitutional consideration to the mere policy, does not this letter imply that the idea of taxing America for the purpose of revenue is an abominable project; when the Ministry suppose that none but factious men, and with seditious views, could charge them with it? does not this letter adopt and sanctify the American distinction of taxing for a revenue? does it not formally reject all future taxation on that principle? does it not state the ministerial rejection of such principle of taxation, not as the occasional, but the constant, opinion of the king's servants? does it not say, I care not how consistently—but does it not say, that their conduct with regard to America has been always governed by this policy? It goes a great deal further. These excellent and trusty servants of the king, justly fearful lest they themselves should have lost all credit with the world, bring out the image of their gracious sovereign from the inmost and most sacred shrine, and they pawn him as a security for their promises—" his Majesty relies on your prudence and fidelity for such an explanation of his measures." These sentiments of the Minister, and these measures of his Majesty, can only relate to the principle and practice of taxing for a revenue; and accordingly Lord Botetourt, stating it as such, did, with great propriety, and in the exact spirit of his instructions, endeavour to remove the fears of the Virginian assembly, lest the sentiments, which it seems— unknown to the world—had always been those of the Ministers, and by which their conduct in respect to America had been governed, should by some possible revolution, favourable to wicked American taxers, be hereafter counteracted. He addresses them in this manner :—

" It may possibly be objected that, as his Majesty's present Administration are not im- mortal, their successors may be inclined to attempt to undo what the present Ministers shall have attempted to perform ; and to that objection I can give but this answer—that it is

my firm opinion that the plan I have stated to
you will certainly take place, and that it will
never be departed from ; and so determined am
I for ever to abide by it, that I will be content
to be declared infamous, if I do not, to the last
hour of my life, at all times, in all places, and
upon all occasions, exert every power with which
I either am or ever shall be legally invested, in
order to obtain and maintain for the continent
of America that satisfaction which I have been
authorized to promise this day, by the confidential servants of our gracious sovereign, who to
my certain knowledge rates his honour so high,
that he would rather part with his crown than
preserve it by deceit."

A glorious and true character! which (since we
suffer his Ministers with impunity to answer for his
ideas of taxation) we ought to make it our business
to enable his Majesty to preserve in all its lustre.
Let him have character, since ours is no more! Let
some part of government be kept in respect!

This epistle was not the letter of Lord Hillsborough solely, though he held the official pen. It
was the letter of the noble lord upon the floor, and
of all the king's then Ministers, who (with I think
the exception of two only) are his Ministers at this
hour. The very first news that a British Parliament
heard of what it was to do with the duties
which it had given and granted to the king,
was by the publication of the votes of American

assemblies. It was in America that your resolutions were pre-declared. It was from thence that we knew to a certainty how much exactly, and not a scruple more or less, we were to repeal. We were unworthy to be let into the secret of our own conduct. The assemblies had confidential communications from his Majesty's confidential servants. We were nothing but instruments. Do you, after this, wonder that you have no weight and no respect in the colonies? After this, you are surprised that Parliament is every day and everywhere losing—I feel it with sorrow, I utter it with reluctance—that reverential affection which so endearing a name of authority ought ever to carry with it; that you are obeyed solely from respect to the bayonet; and that this House, the ground and pillar of freedom, is itself held up only by the treacherous under-pinning and clumsy buttresses of arbitrary power?

If this dignity, which is to stand in the place of just policy and common sense, had been consulted, there was a time for preserving it, and for reconciling it with any concession. If in the session of 1768—that session of idle terror and empty menaces—you had, as you were often pressed to do, repealed these taxes, then your strong operations would have come justified and enforced, in case your concessions had been returned by outrages. But, preposterously, you began with violence; and before terrors could have any effect, either good or bad, your Ministers imme-

diately begged pardon, and promised that repeal to
the obstinate Americans which they had refused in
an easy, good-natured, complying British Parliament. The assemblies which had been publicly and
avowedly dissolved for their contumacy, are called
together to receive your submission. Your ministerial directors blustered like tragic tyrants here ;
and then went mumping with a sore leg in America,
canting and whining, and complaining of faction,
which represented them as friends to a revenue from
the colonies. I hope nobody in this House will
hereafter have the impudence to defend American
taxes in the name of Ministry. The moment they
do, with this letter of attorney in my hand, I will
tell them, in the authorized terms, they are wretches,
"with factious and seditious views ; enemies to the
peace and prosperity of the mother country and the
colonies," and subverters "of the mutual affection
and confidence on which the glory and safety of the
British empire depend."

After this letter, the question is no more on
propriety or dignity. They are gone already. The
faith of your sovereign is pledged for the political
principle. The general declaration in the letter goes
to the whole of it. You must therefore either
abandon the scheme of taxing, or you must send
the Ministers tarred and feathered to America, who
dared to hold out the royal faith for a renunciation
of all taxes for revenue. Them you must punish,

or this faith you must preserve. The preservation of this faith is of more consequence than the duties on red lead, or white lead, or on broken glass, or atlas ordinary, or demy fine, or blue royal, or bastard, or foolscap, which you have given up ; or the three-pence on tea which you retained. The letter went stamped with the public authority of this kingdom. The instructions for the colony government go under no other sanction ; and America cannot believe, and will not obey you, if you do not preserve this channel of communication sacred. You are now punishing the colonies for acting on distinctions, held out by that very Ministry which is here shining in riches, in favour, and in power ; and urging the punishment of the very offence to which they had themselves been the tempters.

Sir, if reasons respecting simply your own commerce, which is your own convenience, were the sole grounds of the repeal of the five duties ; why does Lord Hillsborough, in disclaiming in the name of the King and Ministry their ever having had an intent to tax for revenue, mention it as the means " of re-establishing the confidence and affection of the colonies ? " Is it a way of soothing others, to assure them that you will take good care of yourself ? The medium, the only medium, for regaining their affection and confidence is, that you will take off something oppressive to their minds. Sir, the letter strongly enforces that idea : for though the repeal of

B

the taxes is promised on commercial principles,
yet the means of counteracting "the insinuations of
men with factious and seditious views," is by a disclaimer of the intention of taxing for revenue, as a
constant invariable sentiment and rule of conduct in
the government of America.

I remember that the noble lord on the floor, not
in a former debate to be sure (it would be disorderly
to refer to it—I suppose I read it somewhere), but
the noble lord was pleased to say that he did not
conceive how it could enter into the head of man to
impose such taxes as those of 1767 ; I mean those
taxes which he voted for imposing, and voted for
repealing ; as being taxes contrary to all the principles of commerce, laid on British manufactures.

I daresay the noble lord is perfectly well read,
because the duty of his particular office requires he
should be so, in all our revenue laws, and in the,
policy which is to be collected out of them. Now,
Sir, when he had read this Act of American revenue,
and a little recovered from his astonishment, I
suppose he made one step retrograde (it is but one),
and looked at the Act which stands just before in
the Statute-book. The American Revenue Act is
the forty-fifth chapter ; the other to which I refer is
the forty-fourth of the same session. These two
Acts are both to the same purpose ; both Revenue
Acts ; both taxing out of the kingdom ; and both
taxing British manufactures exported. As the 45th

is an Act for raising a revenue in America, the
44th is an Act for raising a revenue in the Isle of
Man. The two Acts perfectly agree in all respects,
except one. In the Act for taxing the Isle of Man,
the noble lord will find (not, as in the American
Act, four or five articles), but almost the whole body
of British manufactures, taxed from two and a half
to fifteen per cent., and some articles, such as that of
spirits, a great deal higher. You did not think it
uncommercial to tax the whole mass of your manufactures, and, let me add, your agriculture too ; for, I
now recollect, British corn is there also taxed up to
ten per cent., and this too in the very headquarters,
the very citadel of smuggling, the Isle of Man.
Now will the noble lord condescend to tell me why
he repealed the taxes on your manufactures sent out
to America, and not the taxes on the manufactures
exported to the Isle of Man? The principle was
exactly the same, the objects charged infinitely more
extensive, the duties without comparison higher.
Why? Why, notwithstanding all his childish pre-
texts, because the taxes were quietly submitted to in
the Isle of Man, and because they raised a flame in
America. Your reasons were political, not commercial. The repeal was made, as Lord Hillsborough's
letter well expresses it, to regain "the confidence
and affection of the colonies, on which the glory and
safety of the British empire depend." A wise and
just motive surely, if ever there was such. But the

mischief and dishonour is, that you had not done what you had given the colonies just cause to expect, when your Ministers disclaimed the idea of taxes for a revenue. There is nothing simple, nothing manly, nothing ingenuous, open, decisive, or steady, in the proceeding, with regard either to the continuance or the repeal of the taxes. The whole has an air of littleness and fraud. The article of tea is slurred over in the circular letter, as it were by accident—nothing is said of a resolution either to keep that tax, or to give it up. There is no fair dealing in any part of the transaction.

If you mean to follow your true motive and your public faith, give up your tax on tea for raising a revenue, the principle of which has, in effect, been disclaimed in your name, and which produces you no advantage ; no, not a penny. Or, if you choose to go on with a poor pretence instead of a solid reason, and will still adhere to your cant of commerce, you have ten thousand times more strong commercial reasons for giving up this duty on tea, than for abandoning the five others that you have already renounced.

The American consumption of teas is annually, I believe, worth £300,000 at the least farthing. If you urge the American violence as a justification of your perseverance in enforcing this tax, you know that you can never answer this plain question—Why did you repeal the others given in the same Act, whilst the very same violence subsisted? But you did not find the violence cease upon that concession. No! because the concession was far short of satisfying the principle which Lord Hillsborough had abjured ; or even the pretence on which the repeal of the other taxes was announced ; and because, by enabling the East India Company to open a shop for defeating the American resolution not to pay that specific tax, you manifestly showed a hankering after the principle of the Act which you formerly had renounced. Whatever road you take leads to a compliance with this motion. It opens to you at the end of every vista. Your commerce, your policy, your promises, your reasons, your pretences, your consistency, your inconsistency—all jointly oblige you to this repeal.

But still it sticks in our throats, if we go so far, the Americans will go farther. We do not know that. We ought, from experience, rather to presume the contrary. Do we not know for certain that the Americans are going on as fast as possible, whilst we refuse to gratify them? Can they do more, or can they do worse, if we yield this point? I think this concession will rather fix a turnpike to prevent their further progress. It is impossible to answer for bodies of men. But I am sure the natural effect of fidelity, clemency, kindness in governors, is peace, goodwill, order, and esteem on the part of the governed. I would certainly, at least, give these

fair principles a fair trial ; which, since the making
of this Act to this hour, they never have had.

Sir, the honourable gentleman having spoken
what he thought necessary upon the narrow part of
the subject, I have given him, I hope, a satisfactory
answer. He next presses me by a variety of direct
challenges and oblique reflections to say something
on the historical part. I shall therefore, Sir, open
myself fully on that important and delicate subject ;
not for the sake of telling you a long story (which
I know, Mr. Speaker, you are not particularly fond
of), but for the sake of the weighty instruction that,
I flatter myself, will necessarily result from it. I
shall not be longer, if I can help it, than so serious
a matter requires.

Permit me then, Sir, to lead your attention very far
back—back to the Act of Navigation ; the corner-
stone of the policy of this country with regard to its
colonies. Sir, that policy was, from the beginning,
purely commercial, and the commercial system was
wholly restrictive. It was the system of a monopoly.
No trade was let loose from that constraint, but
merely to enable the colonists to dispose of what, in
the course of your trade, you could not take ; or to
enable them to dispose of such articles as we forced
upon them, and for which, without some degree of
liberty, they could not pay. Hence all your specific
and detailed enumerations : hence the innumerable
checks and counter-checks : hence that infinite variety

of paper chains by which you bind together this complicated system of the colonies. This principle of commercial monopoly runs through no less than twenty-nine Acts of Parliament, from the year 1660 to the unfortunate period of 1764.

In all those Acts the system of commerce is established, as that from whence alone you proposed to make the colonies contribute (I mean directly and by the operation of your superintending legislative power) to the strength of the empire. I venture to say, that during that whole period, a parliamentary revenue from thence was never once in contemplation. Accordingly, in all the number of laws passed with regard to the plantations, the words which distinguish revenue laws, specifically as such, were, I think, premeditately avoided. I do not say, Sir, that a form of words alters the nature of the law, or abridges the power of the lawgiver. It certainly does not. However, titles and formal preambles are not always idle words ; and the lawyers frequently argue from them. I state these facts to show, not what was your right, but what has been your settled policy. Our revenue laws have usually a title, purporting their being grants ; and the words "give and grant" usually precede the enacting parts. Although duties were imposed on America in Acts of King Charles the Second and in Acts of King William, no one title of giving "an aid to his Majesty," or any other of the usual titles to Revenue

Acts, was to be found in any of them till 1764 ; nor
were the words "give and grant" in any preamble
until the sixth of George the Second. However,
the title of this Act of George the Second, notwithstanding the words of donation, considers it merely
as a regulation of trade, "An Act for the better
securing of the trade of His Majesty's Sugar Colonies
in America." This Act was made on a compromise
of all, and at the express desire of a part, of the
colonies themselves. It was therefore in some
measure with their consent ; and having a title
directly purporting only a commercial regulation,
and being in truth nothing more, the words were
passed by, at a time when no jealousy was entertained, and things were little scrutinized. Even
Governor Bernard, in his second printed letter, dated
in 1763, gives it as his opinion that "it was an Act of
prohibition, not of revenue." This is certainly true,
that no Act avowedly for the purpose of revenue,
and with the ordinary title and recital taken together,
is found in the Statute-book until the year 1764.
All before this period stood on commercial regulation and restraint. The scheme of a colony revenue
by British authority appeared therefore to the
Americans in the light of a great innovation; the
words of Governor Bernard's ninth letter, written in
Nov. 1765, states this idea very strongly. "It must,"
says he, "have been supposed, such an innovation as
a parliamentary taxation would cause a great alarm,

and meet with much opposition in most parts of America ; it was quite new to the people, and had no visible bounds set to it." After stating the weakness of government there, he says, " Was this a time to introduce so great a novelty as a parliamentary inland taxation in America ?" Whatever the right might have been, this mode of using it was absolutely new in policy and practice.

Sir, they who are friends to the schemes of American revenue say, that the commercial restraint is full as hard a law for America to live under. I think so too. I think it, if uncompensated, to be a condition of as rigorous servitude as men can be subject to. But America bore it from the fundamental Act of Navigation until 1764. Why ? Because men do bear the inevitable constitution of their original nature with all its infirmities. The Act of Navigation attended the colonies from their infancy ; grew with their growth, and strengthened with their strength. They were confirmed in obedience to it, even more by usage than by law. They scarcely had remembered a time when they were not subject to such restraint. Besides, they were indemnified for it by a pecuniary compensation. Their monopolist happened to be one of the richest men in the world. By his immense capital (primarily employed, not for their benefit, but his own) they were enabled to proceed with their fisheries, their agriculture, their ship-building (and their trade too

within the limits), in such a manner as got far the
start of the slow languid operations of unassisted
Nature. This capital was a hot-bed to them.
Nothing in the history of mankind is like their
progress. For my part, I never cast an eye on their
flourishing commerce, and their cultivated and commodious life, but they seem to me rather ancient
nations grown to perfection through a long series of
fortunate events, and a train of successful industry,
accumulating wealth in many centuries, than the
colonies of yesterday ; than a set of miserable out-
casts, a few years ago, not so much sent as thrown out,
on th ebleak and barren shore of a desolate wilderness
three thousand miles from all civilized intercourse.

All this was done by England, whilst England
pursued trade and forgot revenue. You not only
acquired commerce, but you actually created the very
objects of trade in America ; and by that creation
you raised the trade of this kingdom at least fourfold. America had the compensation of your capital,
which made her bear her servitude. She had another
compensation, which you are now going to take
away from her. She had, except the commercial
restraint, every characteristic mark of a free people
in all her internal concerns. She had the image of
the British Constitution. She had the substance.
She was taxed by her own representatives. She
chose most of her own magistrates. She paid them
all. She had in effect the sole disposal of her own

internal government. This whole state of commercial servitude and civil liberty, taken together, is
certainly not perfect freedom ; but comparing it with
the ordinary circumstances of human nature, it was
a happy and a liberal condition.

I know, Sir, that great and not unsuccessful pains
have been taken to inflame our minds by an outcry,
in this House and out of it, that in America the Act
of Navigation neither is, nor ever was, obeyed. But
if you take the colonies through, I affirm that its
authority never was disputed ; that it was nowhere
disputed for any length of time ; and, on the whole,
that it was well observed. Wherever the Act pressed
hard, many individuals indeed evaded it. This is
nothing. These scattered individuals never denied
the law, and never obeyed it. Just as it happens
whenever the laws of trade, whenever the laws of
revenue, press hard upon the people in England—in
that case all your shores are full of contraband.
Your right to give a monopoly to the East India
Company, your right to lay immense duties on French
brandy, are not disputed in England. You do not
make this charge on any man. But you know that
there is not a creek from Pentland Frith to the Isle
of Wight in which they do not smuggle immense
quantities of teas, East India goods, and brandies.
I take it for granted that the authority of Governor
Bernard in this point is indisputable. Speaking of
these laws as they regarded that part of America

now in so unhappy a condition, he says : " I believe
they are nowhere better supported than in this
province ; I do not pretend that it is entirely free
from a breach of these laws ; but that such a breach,
if discovered, is justly punished." What more can
you say of the obedience to any laws in any country?
An obedience to these laws formed the acknowledgment, instituted by yourselves, for your superiority ;
and was the payment you originally imposed for
your protection.

   Whether you were right or wrong in establishing
the colonies on the principles of commercial
monopoly rather than on that of revenue, is at this
day a problem of mere speculation. You cannot
have both by the same authority. To join together
the restraints of a universal internal and external
monopoly, with a universal internal and external
taxation, is an unnatural union—perfect uncompensated slavery. You have long since decided for
yourself and them ; and you and they have prospered
exceedingly under that decision.

   This nation, Sir, never thought of departing from
that choice until the period immediately on the close
of the last war. Then a scheme of government new
in many things, seemed to have been adopted. I
saw, or I thought I saw, several symptoms of a
great change, whilst I sat in your gallery, a good
while before I had the honour of a seat in this
House. At that period the necessity was established

of keeping up no less than twenty new regiments,
with twenty colonels capable of seats in this House.
This scheme was adopted with very general applause
from all sides, at the very time that, by your
conquests in America, your danger from foreign attempts in that part of the world was much lessened,
or indeed rather quite over. When this huge increase of military establishment was resolved on, a
revenue was to be found to support so great a
burthen. Country gentlemen, the great patrons of
economy, and the great resisters of a standing armed
force, would not have entered with much alacrity
into the vote for so large and so expensive an army,
if they had been very sure that they were to
continue to pay for it. But hopes of another kind
were held out to them; and in particular, I well
remember, that Mr. Townshend, in a brilliant
harangue on this subject, did dazzle them by
playing before their eyes the image of a revenue to
be raised in America.

Here began to dawn the first glimmerings of this
new colony system. It appeared more distinctly
afterwards, when it was devolved upon a person to
whom, on other accounts, this country owes very
great obligations. I do believe that he had a very
serious desire to benefit the public. But with no
small study of the detail, he did not seem to have
his view, at least equally, carried to the total circuit
of our affairs. He generally considered his objects

in lights that were rather too detached. Whether the business of an American revenue was imposed upon him altogether; whether it was entirely the result of his own speculation; or, what is more probable, that his own ideas rather coincided with the instructions he had received; certain it is that, with the best intentions in the world, he first brought this fatal scheme into form, and established it by Act of Parliament.

No man can believe that at this time of day I mean to lean on the venerable memory of a great man, whose loss we deplore in common. Our little party differences have been long ago composed; and I have acted more with him, and certainly with more pleasure with him, than ever I acted against him. Undoubtedly Mr. Grenville was a first-rate figure in this country. With a masculine understanding, and a stout and resolute heart, he had an application undissipated and unwearied. He took public business, not as a duty which he was to fulfil, but as a pleasure he was to enjoy; and he seemed to have no delight out of this House, except in such things as some way related to the business that was to be done within it. If he was ambitious, I will say this for him, his ambition was of a noble and generous strain. It was to raise himself, not by the low, pimping politics of a Court, but to win his way to power through the laborious gradations of public service; and to secure to himself a well-earned rank

in Parliament, by a thorough knowledge of its constitution and a perfect practice in all its business.

Sir, if such a man fell into errors, it must be from
defects not intrinsical; they must be rather sought
in the particular habits of his life ; which, though
they do not alter the groundwork of character, yet
tinge it with their own hue. He was bred in a profession. He was bred to the law, which is, in my
opinion, one of the first and noblest of human
sciences—a science which does more to quicken and
invigorate the understanding than all the other
kinds of learning put together; but it is not apt,
except in persons very happily born, to open and to
liberalize the mind exactly in the same proportion.
Passing from that study he did not go very largely
into the world ; but plunged into business—I mean
into the business of office and the limited and fixed
methods and forms established there. Much knowledge is to be had undoubtedly in that line, and there
is no knowledge which is not valuable. But it may
be truly said that men too much conversant in office
are rarely minds of remarkable enlargement. Their
habits of office are apt to give them a turn to think
the substance of business not to be much more important than the forms in which it is conducted.
These forms are adapted to ordinary occasions, and
therefore persons who are nurtured in office do
admirably well as long as things go on in their
common order ; but when the high roads are broken

up, and the waters out—when a new and troubled
scene is opened, and the file affords no precedent—
then it is that a greater knowledge of mankind, and
a far more extensive comprehension of things, is
requisite than ever office gave, or than office can
ever give. Mr. Grenville thought better of the
wisdom and power of human legislation than in
truth it deserves. He conceived, and many conceived
along with him, that the flourishing trade of this
country was greatly owing to law and institution,
and not quite so much to liberty ; for but too many
are apt to believe regulation to be commerce, and taxes
to be revenue. Among regulations, that which stood
first in reputation was his idol. I mean the Act of
Navigation. He has often professed it to be so.
The policy of that Act is, I readily admit, in many
respects, well understood. But I do say, that if the
Act be suffered to run the full length of its principle,
and is not changed and modified according to the
change of times and the fluctuation of circumstances,
it must do great mischief, and frequently even defeat
its own purpose.

After the war, and in the last years of it, the trade
of America had increased far beyond the speculations
of the most sanguine imaginations. It swelled out
on every side. It filled all its proper channels to
the brim. It overflowed with a rich redundance,
and, breaking its banks on the right and on the left,
it spread out upon some places where it was indeed

improper, upon others where it was only irregular.
It is the nature of all greatness not to be exact ; and
great trade will always be attended with considerable
abuses. The contraband will always keep pace in
some measure with the fair trade. It should stand
as a fundamental maxim, that no vulgar precaution
ought to be employed in the cure of evils which are
closely connected with the cause of our prosperity.
Perhaps this great person turned his eyes somewhat
less than was just towards the incredible increase of
the fair trade, and looked with something of too
exquisite a jealousy towards the contraband. He
certainly felt a singular degree of anxiety on the
subject, and even began to act from that passion
earlier than is commonly imagined. For whilst he
was First Lord of the Admiralty, though not strictly
called upon in his official line, he presented a very
strong memorial to the Lords of the Treasury (my
Lord Bute was then at the head of the board), heavily
complaining of the growth of the illicit commerce in
America. Some mischief happened even at that
time from this over-earnest zeal. Much greater happened afterwards, when it operated with greater
power in the highest department of the finances.
The bonds of the Act of Navigation were straitened
so much, that America was on the point of having
no trade, either contraband or legitimate. They
found, under the construction and execution then
used, the Act no longer tying, but actually strangling

them. All this coming with new enumerations of commodities ; with regulations which in a manner put a stop to the mutual coasting intercourse of the colonies ; with the appointment of Courts of Admiralty under various improper circumstances ; with a sudden extinction of the paper currencies ; with a compulsory provision for the quartering of soldiers ; the people of America thought themselves proceeded against as delinquents, or, at best, as people under suspicion of delinquency; and in such a manner as, they imagined, their recent services in the war did not at all merit. Any of these innumerable regulations, perhaps, would not have alarmed alone ; some might be thought reasonable ; the multitude struck them with terror.

But the grand manœuvre in that business of new regulating the colonies, was the 15th Act of the fourth of George the Third ; which, besides containing several of the matters to which I have just alluded, opened a new principle ; and here properly began the second period of the policy of this country with regard to the colonies ; by which the scheme of a regular plantation parliamentary revenue was adopted in theory, and settled in practice. A revenue not substituted in the place of, but superadded to, a monopoly ; which monopoly was enforced at the same time with additional strictness, and the execution put into military hands.

This Act, Sir, had for the first time the title of

"granting duties in the colonies and plantations of America ;" and for the first time it was asserted in the preamble, "that it was just and necessary that a revenue should be raised there." Then came the technical words of "giving and granting ;" and thus a complete American Revenue Act was made in all the forms, and with a full avowal of the right, equity, policy, and even necessity of taxing the colonies, without any formal consent of theirs. There are contained also in the preamble to that Act these very remarkable words—the Commons, &c.—" being desirous to make some provision in the present session of Parliament towards raising the said revenue." By these words it appeared to the colonies that this Act was but a beginning of sorrows ; that every session was to produce something of the same kind ; that we were to go on, from day to day, in charging them with such taxes as we pleased, for such a military force as we should think proper. Had this plan been pursued, it was evident that the provincial assemblies, in which the Americans felt all their portion of importance, and beheld their sole image of freedom, were *ipso facto* annihilated. This .ll prospect before them seemed to be boundless in extent, and endless in duration. Sir, they were not mistaken. The Ministry valued themselves when this Act passed, and when they gave notice of the Stamp Act, that both of the duties came very short of their ideas of American taxation. Great was the

applause of this measure here.   In England we cried
out for new taxes on America, whilst they cried out
that they were nearly crushed with those which the
war   and   their   own   grants   had   brought   upon
them.

Sir, it has been said in the debate, that when the
first American Revenue Act (the Act in 1764 imposing the port duties) passed, the Americans did not
object to the principle.   It is true they touched it
but very tenderly.   It was not a direct attack.
They were, it is true, as yet novices ; as yet unaccus-
tomed to direct attacks upon any of the rights of
Parliament.   The duties were port duties, like those
they had been accustomed to bear ; with this difference, that the title was not the same, the preamble
not the same, and the spirit altogether unlike.   But
of what service is this observation to the cause of
those that make it ?   It is a full refutation of the
pretence for their present cruelty to America ; for
it shows, out of their own mouths, that our colonies
were backward to enter into the present vexatious
and ruinous controversy.

There is also another circulation abroad (spread
with a malignant intention, which I cannot attribute
to those who say the same thing in this House), that
Mr. Grenville gave the colony agents an option for
their assemblies to tax themselves, which they had
refused.   I find that much stress is laid on this, as a
fact.   However, it happens neither to be true nor

possible. I will observe, first, that Mr. Grenville
never thought fit to make this apology for himself
in the innumerable debates that were had upon the
subject. He might have proposed to the colony
agents that they should agree in some mode of
taxation as the ground of an Act of Parliament.
But he never could have proposed that they should
tax themselves on requisition, which is the assertion
of the day. Indeed, Mr. Grenville well knew that
the colony agents could have no general powers to
consent to it ; and they had no time to consult their
assemblies for particular powers, before he passed
his first Revenue Act. If you compare dates, you
will find it impossible. Burthened as the agents
knew the colonies were at that time, they could
not give the least hope of such grants. His own
favourite governor was of opinion that the Americans
were not then taxable objects.

"Nor was the time less favourable to the
equity of such a taxation. I don't mean to
dispute the reasonableness of America contributing to the charges of Great Britain when
she is able ; nor, I believe, would the Americans
themselves have disputed it, at a proper time
and season. But it should be considered that
the American governments themselves have, in
the prosecution of the late war, contracted very
large debts, which it will take some years to
pay off, and in the meantime occasion very
burdensome taxes for that purpose only. For

instance, this government, which is as much beforehand as any, raises every year £37,500 sterling for sinking their debt, and must continue it for four years longer at least before it will be clear."

These are the words of Governor Bernard's letter to a member of the old Ministry, and which he has since printed. Mr. Grenville could not have made this proposition to the agents, for another reason. He was of opinion, which he has declared in this House a hundred times, that the colonies could not legally grant any revenue to the Crown; and that infinite mischiefs would be the consequence of such a power. When Mr. Grenville had passed the first Revenue Act, and in the same session had made this House come to a resolution for laying a stamp duty on America, between that time and the passing the Stamp Act into a law, he told a considerable and most respectable merchant, a member of this House, whom I am truly sorry I do not now see in his place, when he represented against this proceeding, that if the stamp duty was disliked, he was willing to exchange it for any other equally productive; but that, if he objected to the Americans being taxed by Parliament, he might save himself the trouble of the discussion, as he was determined on the measure. This is the fact, and, if you please, I will mention a very unquestionable authority for it.

Thus, Sir, I have disposed of this falsehood. But falsehood has a perennial spring. It is said that no conjecture could be made of the dislike of the colonies to the principle. This is as untrue as the other. After the resolution of the House, and before the passing of the Stamp Act, the colonies of Massachusetts Bay and New York did send remonstrances, objecting to this mode of parliamentary taxation. What was the consequence? They were suppressed; they were put under the table, notwithstanding an order of Council to the contrary, by the Ministry which composed the very Council that had made the order: and thus the House proceeded to its business of taxing without the least regular knowledge of the objections which were made to it. But to give that House its due, it was not over-desirous to receive information, or to hear remonstrance. On the 15th of February, 1765, whilst the Stamp Act was under deliberation, they refused with scorn even so much as to receive four petitions presented from so respectable colonies as Connecticut, Rhode Island, Virginia, and Carolina ; besides one from the traders of Jamaica. As to the colonies, they had no alternative left to them but to disobey, or to pay the taxes imposed by that Parliament which was not suffered, or did not suffer itself, even to hear them remonstrate upon the subject.

This was the state of the colonies before his Majesty thought fit to change his Ministers. It stands upon no authority of mine. It is proved by incontrovertible records. The honourable gentleman has desired some of us to lay our hands upon our hearts, and answer to his queries upon the historical part of this consideration ; and by his manner (as well as my eyes could discern it) he seemed to address himself to me.

Sir, I will answer him as clearly as I am able, and with great openness ; I have nothing to conceal. In the year sixty-five, being in a very private station, far enough from any line of business, and not having the honour of a seat in this House, it was my fortune, unknowing and unknown to the then Ministry, by the intervention of a common friend, to become connected with a very noble person, and at the head of the Treasury department. It was indeed in a situation of little rank and no consequence, suitable to the mediocrity of my talents and pretensions. But a situation near enough to enable me to see, as well as others, what was going on ; and I did see in that noble person such sound principles, such an enlargement of mind, such clear and sagacious sense, and such unshaken fortitude, as have bound me, as well as others much better than me, by an inviolable attachment to him from that time forward. Sir, Lord Rockingham very early in that summer received a strong representation from many weighty English merchants and manufacturers, from governors of provinces and commanders of men-of-war, against almost the whole of the American commercial regulations; and particularly with regard to the total ruin which was threatened to the Spanish trade. I believe, Sir, the noble lord soon saw his way in this business. But he did not rashly determine against Acts which it might be supposed were the result of much deliberation. However, Sir, he scarcely began to open the ground when the whole veteran body of office took the alarm. A violent outcry of all (except those who knew and felt the mischief) was raised against any alteration. On one hand, his attempt was a direct violation of treaties and public law; on the other, the Act of Navigation and all the corps of trade laws were drawn up in array against it.

The first step the noble lord took was to have the opinion of his excellent, learned, and ever-lamented friend, the late Mr. Yorke, then Attorney-General, on the point of law. When he knew that formally and officially, which in substance he had known before, he immediately despatched orders to redress the grievance. But I will say it for the then Minister, he is of that constitution of mind that I know he would have issued, on the same critical occasion, the very same orders if the Acts of trade had been, as they were not, directly against him; and would have cheerfully submitted to the equity of Parliament for his indemnity.

On the conclusion of this business of the Spanish

trade, the news of the troubles on account of the
Stamp Act arrived in England.   It was not until the
end of October that these accounts were received.
No sooner had the sound of that mighty tempest
reached us in England, than the whole of the then
opposition, instead of feeling humbled by the unhappy
issue of their measures, seemed to be infinitely elated,
and cried out that the Ministry, from envy to the
glory of their predecessors, were prepared to repeal
the Stamp Act.   Near nine years after, the honourable gentleman takes quite opposite ground, and
now challenges me to put my hand to my heart, and
say whether the Ministry had resolved on the repeal
till a considerable time after the meeting of Parliament.   Though I do not very well know what the
honourable gentleman wishes to infer from the
admission, or from the denial, of this fact, on which
he so earnestly adjures me, I do put my hand on
my heart, and assure him that they did not come to
a resolution directly to repeal.   They weighed this
matter as its difficulty and importance required.
They considered maturely among themselves.   They
consulted with all who could give advice or information.   It was not determined until a little before the
meeting of Parliament ; but it was determined, and
the main lines of their own plan marked out, before
that meeting.   Two questions arose—I hope I am
not going into a narrative troublesome to the
House—the first of the two considerations was,

whether the repeal should be total, or whether only partial ; taking out everything burthensome and productive, and reserving only an empty acknowledgment, such as a stamp on cards or dice. The other question was, on what principle the Act should be repealed ? On this head also two principles were started. One, that the legislative rights of this country, with regard to America, were not entire, but had certain restrictions and limitations. The other principle was, that taxes of this kind were contrary to the fundamental principles of commerce on which the colonies were founded, and contrary to every idea of political equity ; by which equity we are bound, as much as possible, to extend the spirit and benefit of the British Constitution to every part of the British dominions. The option, both of the measure and of the principle of repeal, was made before the session ; and I wonder how any one can read the King's Speech at the opening of that session without seeing in that speech both the repeal and the Declaratory Act very sufficiently crayoned out. Those who cannot see this, can see nothing.

Surely the honourable gentleman will not think that a great deal less time than was then employed ought to have been spent in deliberation, when he considers that the news of the troubles did not arrive till towards the end of October. The Parliament sat to fill the vacancies on the 14th day of December, and on business the 14th of the following January.

Sir, a partial repeal, or, as the *bon ton* of the Court
then was, a modification, would have satisfied a
timid, unsystematic, procrastinating Ministry, as
such a measure has since done such a Ministry.   A
modification is the constant resource of weak,
undeciding minds.   To repeal by the denial of our
right to tax in the preamble (and this too did not
want advisers), would have cut, in the heroic style,
the Gordian knot with a sword.   Either measure
would have cost no more than a day's debate.   But
when the total repeal was adopted—and adopted on
principles of policy, of equity, and of commerce—this
plan made it necessary to enter into many and
difficult measures.   It became necessary to open a
very large field of evidence commensurate to these
extensive views.   But then this labour did knight's
service.   It opened the eyes of several to the true
state of the American affairs ; it enlarged their
ideas ; it removed prejudices ; and it conciliated the
opinions and affections of men.   The noble lord, who
then took the lead in administration, my honourable
friend under me, and a right honourable gentleman
(if he will not reject his share, and it was a large
one, of this business), exerted the most laudable
industry in bringing before you the fullest, most
impartial, and least garbled body of evidence that
ever was produced to this House.   I think the
inquiry lasted in the committee for six weeks ; and,
at its conclusion, this House, by an independent,

noble, spirited, and unexpected majority ; by a majority that will redeem all the acts ever done by majorities in Parliament ; in the teeth of all the old mercenary Swiss of state, in despite of all the speculators and augurs of political events, in defiance of the whole embattled legion of veteran pensioners and practised instruments of a Court, gave a total repeal to the Stamp Act, and (if it had been so per- mitted) a lasting peace to this whole empire.

I state, Sir, these particulars, because this act of spirit and fortitude has lately been, in the circulation of the season, and in some hazarded declamations in this House, attributed to timidity. If, Sir, the con-duct of Ministry, in proposing the repeal, had arisen from timidity with regard to themselves, it would have been greatly to be condemned. Interested timidity disgraces as much in the Cabinet as personal timidity does in the field. But timidity, with regard to the well-being of our country, is heroic virtue. The noble lord who then conducted affairs, and his worthy colleagues, whilst they trembled at the prospect of such distresses as you have since brought upon yourselves, were not afraid steadily to look in the face that glaring and dazzling influence at which the eyes of eagles have blenched. He looked in the face one of the ablest, and, let me say, not the most scrupulous, Oppositions that perhaps ever was in this House ; and withstood it, unaided by even one of the usual supports of administration. He did this when he repealed the Stamp Act. He looked in the face a person he had long respected and regarded, and whose aid was then particularly wanting—I mean Lord Chatham. He did this when he passed the Declaratory Act.

It is now given out for the usual purposes by the usual emissaries, that Lord Rockingham did not consent to the repeal of this Act until he was bullied into it by Lord Chatham ; and the reporters have gone so far as publicly to assert, in a hundred companies, that the honourable gentleman under the gallery, who proposed the repeal in the American committee, had another set of resolutions in his pocket directly the reverse of those he moved. These artifices of a desperate cause are at this time spread abroad, with incredible care, in every part of the town, from the highest to the lowest companies ; as if the industry of the circulation were to make amends for the absurdity of the report.

Sir, whether the noble lord is of a complexion to be bullied by Lord Chatham, or by any man, I must submit to those who know him. I confess, when I look back to that time, I consider him as placed in one of the most trying situations in which, perhaps, any man ever stood. In the House of Peers there were very few of the Ministry, out of the noble lord's own particular connection (except Lord Egmont, who acted, as far as I could discern, an honourable and manly part), that did not look to some other future arrangement, which warped his politics. There were in both Houses new and menacing appearances, that might very naturally drive any other than a most resolute Minister from his measure or from his station. The household troops openly revolted. The allies of Ministry (those, I mean, who supported some of their measures, but refused responsibility for any) endeavoured to undermine their credit, and to take ground that must be fatal to the success of the very cause which they would be thought to countenance. The question of the repeal was brought on by Ministry in the Committee of this House, in the very instant when it was known that more than one Court negotiation was carrying on with the heads of the Opposition. Everything upon every side, was full of traps and mines. Earth below shook; heaven above menaced; all the elements of ministerial safety were dissolved. It was in the midst of this chaos of plots and counter-plots—it was in the midst of this complicated warfare against public opposition and private treachery, that the firmness of that noble person was put to the proof. He never stirred from his ground; no, not an inch. He remained fixed and determined, in principle, in measure, and in conduct. He practised no managements. He secured no retreat. He sought no apology.

I will likewise do justice—I ought to do it—to the honourable gentleman who led us in this House.

Far from the duplicity wickedly charged on him, he acted his part with alacrity and resolution. We all felt inspired by the example he gave us, down even to myself, the weakest in that phalanx. I declare for one, I knew well enough (it could not be concealed from anybody) the true state of things ; but in my life I never came with so much spirits into this House. It was a time for a man to act in. We had powerful enemies ; but we had faithful and determined friends, and a glorious cause. We had a great battle to fight ; but we had the means of fighting, not as now, when our arms are tied behind us. We did fight that day, and conquer.

I remember, Sir, with a melancholy pleasure, the situation of the honourable gentleman who made the motion for the repeal ; in that crisis, when the whole trading interest of this empire, crammed into your lobbies, with a trembling and anxious expectation, waited, almost to a winter's return of light, their fate from your resolutions. When at length you had determined in their favour, and your doors, thrown open, showed them the figure of their deliverer in the well-earned triumph of his important victory, from the whole of that grave multitude there arose an involuntary burst of gratitude and transport. They jumped upon him like children on a long absent father. They clung about him as captives about their redeemer. All England, all America, joined to his applause. Nor did he seem

insensible to the best of all earthly rewards—the
love and admiration of his fellow-citizens. Hope
elevated and joy brightened his crest. I stood near
him, and his face—to use the expression of the
Scripture of the first martyr—his face was as if it
had been the face of an angel. I do not know how
others feel; but if I had stood in that situation,
I never would have exchanged it for all that kings
in their profusion could bestow. I did hope that
that day's danger and honour would have been a
bond to hold us all together for ever. But, alas !
that, with other pleasing visions, is long since
vanished.

Sir, this act of supreme magnanimity has been
represented as if it had been a measure of an
Administration that, having no scheme of their
own, took a middle line, pilfered a bit from one
side and a bit from the other. Sir, they took no
middle lines. They differed fundamentally from the
schemes of both parties, but they preserved the
objects of both. They preserved the authority of
Great Britain ; they preserved the equity of Great
Britain ; they made the Declaratory Act ; they
repealed the Stamp Act. They did both fully,
because the Declaratory Act was without qualification, and the repeal of the Stamp Act total.
This they did in the situation I have described.

Now, Sir, what will the adversary say to both
these Acts ? If the principle of the Declaratory

C

Act was not good, the principle we are contending
for this day is monstrous. If the principle of the
repeal was not good, why are we not at war for a
real, substantial, effective revenue ? If both were
bad, why has this Ministry incurred all the inconveniences of both and of all schemes? Why have
they enacted, repealed, enforced, yielded, and now
attempt to enforce again ?

Sir, I think I may as well now, as at any other
time, speak to a certain matter of fact, not wholly
unrelated to the question under your consideration.
We, who would persuade you to revert to the
ancient policy of this kingdom, labour under the
effect of this short current phrase, which the Court
leaders have given out to all their corps, in order
to take away the credit of those who would prevent
you from that frantic war you are going to wage
upon your colonies. Their cant is this : " All the
disturbances in America have been created by the
repeal of the Stamp Act." I suppress for a moment
my indignation at the falsehood, baseness and
absurdity of this most audacious assertion. Instead
of remarking on the motives and character of those
who have issued it for circulation, I will clearly lay
before you the state of America antecedently to that
repeal, after the repeal, and since the renewal of the
schemes of American taxation.

It is said that the disturbances, if there were
any, before the repeal were slight, and without

difficulty or inconvenience might have been suppressed. For an answer to this assertion I will
send you to the great author and patron of the
Stamp Act, who, certainly meaning well to the
authority of this country, and fully apprised of the
state of that, made, before a repeal was so much
as agitated in this House, the motion which is on
your Journals, and which, to save the clerk the
trouble of turning to it, I will now read to you.
It was for an amendment to the Address of the
17th of December 1765 :—

"To express our just resentment and indignation at the outrages, tumults and insurrections
which have been excited and carried on in
North America, and at the resistance given by
open and rebellious force to the execution of
the laws in that part of his Majesty's dominions;
and to assure his Majesty that his faithful
Commons, animated with the warmest duty and
attachment to his royal person and government,
will firmly and effectually support his Majesty
in all such measures as shall be necessary for
preserving and supporting the legal dependence
of the colonies on the mother country," &c. &c.

Here was certainly a disturbance preceding the
repeal ; such a disturbance as Mr. Grenville thought
necessary to qualify by the name of an insurrection
and the epithet of a rebellious force—terms much
stronger than any by which those who then supported

C 2

his motion have ever since thought proper to distinguish the subsequent disturbances in America. They were disturbances which seemed to him and his friends to justify as strong a promise of support as hath been usual to give in the beginning of a war with the most powerful and declared enemies. When the accounts of the American governors came before the House, they appeared stronger even than the warmth of public imagination had painted them; so much stronger that the papers on your table bear me out in saying that all the late disturbances, which have been at one time the Minister's motives for the repeal of five out of six of the new Court taxes, and are now his pretences for refusing to repeal that sixth, did not amount—why do I compare them?—no, not to a tenth part of the tumults and violence which prevailed long before the repeal of that Act.

Ministry cannot refuse the authority of the Commander-in-Chief, General Gage, who, in his letter of the 4th of November, from New York, thus represents the state of things :—

"It is difficult to say, from the highest to the lowest, who has not been accessory to this insurrection, either by writing or mutual agreements, to oppose the Act, by what they are pleased to term all legal opposition to it. Nothing effectual has been proposed, either to prevent or quell the tumult. The rest of the provinces are in the same situation as to a

positive refusal to take the stamps, and threaten-
ing those who shall take them, to plunder and
murder them ; and this affair stands in all the
provinces, that unless the Act, from its own
nature, enforce itself, nothing but a very considerable military force can do it."

It is remarkable, Sir, that the persons who formerly trumpeted forth the most loudly the violent
resolutions of assembles ; the universal insurrections ;
the seizing and burning the stamped papers ; the
forcing stamp officers to resign their commissions
under the gallows ; the rifling and pulling down the
houses of magistrates ; and the expulsion from their
country of all who dared to write or speak a single
word in defence of the powers of Parliament ; these
very trumpeters are now the men that represent the
whole as a mere trifle, and choose to date all the
disturbances from the repeal of the Stamp Act, which
put an end to them.   Hear your officers abroad,
and let them refute this shameless falsehood, who, in
all their correspondence, state the disturbances as
owing to their true causes, the discontent of the
people, from the taxes.   You have this evidence in
your own archives—and it will give you complete
satisfaction, if you are not so far lost to all
parliamentary ideas of information as rather to
credit the lie of the day than the records of your
own House.

Sir, this vermin of Court reporters, when they are

forced into day upon one point, are sure to burrow
in another; but they shall have no refuge; I will
make them bolt out of all their holes. Conscious
that they must be baffled, when they attribute a
precedent disturbance to a subsequent measure, they
take other ground almost as absurd, but very
common in modern practice, and very wicked;
which is, to attribute the ill effect of ill-judged
conduct to the arguments which had been used to
dissuade us from it. They say that the opposition
made in Parliament to the Stamp Act at the time
of its passing, encouraged the Americans to their
resistance. This has even formally appeared in
print in a regular volume, from an advocate of that
faction, a Dr. Tucker. This Dr. Tucker is already
a dean, and his earnest labours in this vineyard will,
I suppose, raise him to a bishopric. But this assertion too, just like the rest, is false. In all the
papers which have loaded your table; in all the vast
crowd of verbal witnesses that appeared at your bar
—witnesses which were indiscriminately produced
from both sides of the House—not the least hint of
such a cause of disturbance has ever appeared. As
to the fact of a strenuous opposition to the Stamp
Act, I sat as a stranger in your gallery when the
Act was under consideration. Far from anything
inflammatory, I never heard a more languid debate
in this House. No more than two or three gentlemen, as I remember, spoke against the Act, and

that with great reserve and remarkable temper. There was but one division in the whole progress of the Bill, and the minority did not reach to more than 39 or 40. In the House of Lords, I do not recollect that there was any debate or division at all. I am sure there was no protest. In fact, the affair passed with so very, very little noise, that in town they scarcely knew the nature of what you were doing. The opposition to the Bill in England never could have done this mischief, because there scarcely ever was less of opposition to a Bill of consequence.

Sir, the agents and distributors of falsehoods have, with their usual industry, circulated another lie of the same nature with the former. It is this, that the disturbances arose from the account which had been received in America of the change in the Ministry. No longer awed, it seems, with the spirit of the former rulers, they thought themselves a match for what our calumniators chose to qualify by the name of so feeble a Ministry as succeeded. Feeble in one sense these men certainly may be called ; for, with all their efforts—and they have made many—they have not been able to resist the distempered vigour and insane alacrity with which you are rushing to your ruin. But it does so happen that the falsity of this circulation is (like the rest) demonstrated by indisputable dates and records.

So little was the change known in America, that

the letters of your governors, giving an account of these disturbances long after they had arrived at their highest pitch, were all directed to the old Ministry, and particularly to the Earl of Halifax, the Secretary of State corresponding with the colonies, without once in the smallest degree intimating the slightest suspicion of any ministerial revolution whatsoever. The Ministry was not changed in England until the 10th day of July 1765. On the 14th of the preceding June, Governor Fauquier from Virginia writes thus—and writes thus to the Earl of Halifax :—

> "Government is set at defiance, not having strength enough in her hands to enforce obedience to the laws of the community. The private distress, which every man feels, increases the general dissatisfaction at the duties laid by the Stamp Act, which breaks out and shows itself upon every trifling occasion."

The general dissatisfaction had produced some time before—that is, on the 29th of May—several strong public resolves against the Stamp Act ; and those resolves are assigned by Governor Bernard as the cause of the insurrections in Massachusetts Bay, in his letter of the 15th of August, still addressed to the Earl of Halifax ; and he continued to address such accounts to that Minister quite to the 7th of September of the same year. Similar accounts, and of as late a date, were sent from other governors, and all directed, to Lord Halifax. Not one of these letters indicates the slightest idea of a change, either known, or even apprehended.

Thus are blown away the insect race of courtly falsehoods! thus perish the miserable inventions of the wretched runners for a wretched cause, which they have fly-blown into every weak and rotten part of the country, in vain hopes that when their maggots had taken wing their importunate buzzing might sound something like the public voice!

Sir, I have troubled you sufficiently with the state of America before the repeal. Now I turn to the honourable gentleman who so stoutly challenges us to tell, whether, after the repeal, the provinces were quiet? This is coming home to the point. Here I meet him directly; and answer most readily, they were quiet. And I, in my turn, challenge him to prove when, and where, and by whom, and in what numbers, and with what violence, the other laws of trade, as gentlemen assert, were violated in consequence of your concession? or that even your other revenue laws were attacked? But I quit the vantage-ground on which I stand, and where I might leave the burthen of the proof upon him: I walk down upon the open plain, and undertake to show that they were not only quiet, but showed many unequivocal marks of acknowledgment and gratitude. And to give him every advantage, I select the obnoxious colony of Massachusetts Bay, which at this time (but without hearing her) is so heavily a culprit before Parliament—I will select their proceedings even under circumstances of no small irritation. For, a little imprudently, I must say, Governor Bernard mixed in the administration of the lenitive of a repeal no small acrimony arising from matters of a separate nature. Yet see, Sir, the effect of that lenitive, though mixed with these bitter ingredients, and how this rugged people can express themselves on a measure of concession :

> " If it is not in our power " (say they in their address to Governor Bernard), " in so full a manner as will be expected, to show our respectful gratitude to the mother country, or to make a dutiful and affectionate return to the indulgence of the King and Parliament, it shall be no fault of ours ; for this we intend, and hope we shall be able fully to effect."

Would to God that this temper had been cultivated, managed, and set in action ! Other effects than those which we have since felt would have resulted from it. On the requisition for compensation to those who had suffered from the violence of the populace, in the same address they say :

> " The recommendation enjoined by Mr. Secretary Conway's letter, and in consequence thereof made to us, we will embrace the first convenient opportunity to consider and act upon."

They did consider ; they did act upon it. They
obeyed the requisition. I know the mode has been
chicaned upon ; but it was substantially obeyed ; and
much better obeyed than I fear the parliamentary
requisition of this session will be, though enforced
by all your rigour and backed with all your power.
In a word, the damages of popular fury were com-
pensated by legislative gravity. Almost every other
part of America in various ways demonstrated their
gratitude. I am bold to say, that so sudden a calm
recovered after so violent a storm is without parallel
in history. To say that no other disturbance should
happen from any other cause, is folly. But as far
as appearances went, by the judicious sacrifice of one
law you procured an acquiescence in all that
remained. After this experience, nobody shall
persuade me, when a whole people are concerned,
that acts of lenity are not means of conciliation.

I hope the honourable gentleman has received a
fair and full answer to his question.

I have done with the third period of your policy—
that of your repeal ; and the return of your ancient
system, and your ancient tranquillity and concord.
Sir, this period was not as long as it was happy.
Another scene was opened, and other actors appeared
on the stage. The State, in the condition I have
described it, was delivered into the hands of Lord
Chatham—a great and celebrated name ; a name
that keeps the name of this country respectable

in every other on the globe. It may be truly
called,

Clarum et venerabile nomen
Gentibus, et multum nostræ quod proderat urbi.

Sir, the venerable age of this great man, his
merited rank, his superior eloquence, his splendid
qualities, his eminent services, the vast space he fills
in the eye of mankind—and, more than all the rest,
his fall from power, which, like death, canonizes and
sanctifies a great character—will not suffer me to
censure any part of his conduct.   I am afraid to
flatter him ; I am sure I am not disposed to blame
him.   Let those who have betrayed him by their
adulation, insult him with their malevolence.   But
what I do not presume to censure, I may have leave
to lament.   For a wise man, he seemed to me at
that time to be governed too much by general
maxims.   I speak with the freedom of history, and .
I hope without offence.   One or two of these
maxims, flowing from an opinion not the most
indulgent to our unhappy species, and surely a little
too general, led him into measures that were greatly
mischievous to himself ; and for that reason, among
others, perhaps fatal to his country ; measures, the
effects of which, I am afraid, are for ever incurable.
He made an administration, so chequered and
speckled ; he put together a piece of joinery, so
crossly indented and whimsically dovetailed ; a
cabinet so variously inlaid ; such a piece of diversi-

fied mosaic ; such a tesselated pavement without cement—here a bit of black stone, and there a bit of white ; patriots and courtiers, King's friends and Republicans ; Whigs and Tories ; treacherous friends and open enemies ; that it was indeed a very curious show ; but utterly unsafe to touch, and unsure to stand on. The colleagues whom he had assorted at the same boards, stared at each other, and were obliged to ask, " Sir, your name ? "—" Sir, you have the advantage of me "—" Mr. Such-a-one "--" I beg a thousand pardons ; " I venture to say, it did so happen, that persons had a single office divided between them, who had never spoke to each other in their lives, until they found themselves, they knew not how, pigging together, heads and points, in the same truckle-bed.

Sir, in consequence of this arrangement, having ·put· so much the larger part of his enemies and opposers into power, the confusion was such that his own principles could not possibly have any effect or influence in the conduct of affairs. If ever he fell into a fit of the gout, or if any other cause withdrew him from public cares, principles directly the contrary were sure to predominate. When he had executed his plan, he had not an inch of ground to stand upon. When he had accomplished his scheme of administration, he was no longer a Minister.

When his face was hid but for a moment, his

whole system was on a wide sea, without chart or compass. The gentlemen, his particular friends, who, with the names of various departments of Ministry, were admitted to seem as if they acted a part under him, with a modesty that becomes all men, and with a confidence in him which was justified, even in its extravagance, by his superior abilities, had never, in any instance, presumed upon any opinion of their own. Deprived of his guiding influence, they were whirled about, the sport of every gust, and easily driven into any port ; and as those who joined with them in manning the vessel were the most directly opposite to his opinions, measures, and character, and far the most artful and most powerful of the set, they easily prevailed, so as to seize upon the vacant, unoccupied, and derelict minds of his friends ; and instantly they turned the vessel wholly out of the course of his policy. As if it were to insult as well as to betray him, even long before the close of the first session of his administration, when everything was publicly transacted, and with great parade, in his name, they made an Act, declaring it highly just and expedient to raise a . revenue in America. For even then, Sir, even before this splendid orb was entirely set, and while the Western horizon was in a blaze with his descending glory, on the opposite quarter of the heavens arose another luminary, and, for his hour, became lord of the ascendant.

This light too is passed and set for ever. You understand, to be sure, that I speak of Charles Townshend, officially the reproducer of this fatal scheme, whom I cannot even now remember without some degree of sensibility. In truth, Sir, he was the delight and ornament of this House, and the charm of every private society which he honoured with his presence. Perhaps there never arose in this country, nor in any country, a man of a more pointed and finished wit ; and (where his passions were not concerned) of a more refined, exquisite, and penetrating judgment. If he had not so great a stock, as some have had who flourished formerly, of knowledge long treasured up, he knew better by far than any man I ever was acquainted with how to bring together, within a short time, all that was necessary to establish, to illustrate, and to decorate that side of the question he supported. He stated his matter skilfully and powerfully. He particularly excelled in a most luminous explanation and display of his subject. His style of argument was neither trite and vulgar, nor subtle and abstruse. He hit the House just between wind and water. And not being troubled with too anxious a zeal for any matter in question, he was never more tedious or more earnest than the preconceived opinions and present temper of his hearers required, to whom he was always in perfect unison. He conformed exactly to the temper of the House ;

and he seemed to guide, because he was also sure
to follow it.

I beg pardon, Sir, if, when I speak of this and of
other great men, I appear to digress in saying
something of their characters.   In this eventful
history of the revolutions of America, the characters
of such men are of much importance.   Great men
are the guide-posts and land-marks in the State.
The credit of such men at Court, or in the nation, is
the sole cause of all the public measures.   It would
be an invidious thing (most foreign, I trust, to what
you think my disposition) to remark the errors into
which the authority of great names has brought the
nation, without doing justice at the same time to
the great qualities whence that authority arose.
The subject is instructive to those who wish to form
themselves on whatever of excellence has gone before
them.   There are many young members in the
House (such of late has been the rapid succession of
public men) who never saw that prodigy, Charles
Townshend ; nor of course know what a ferment he
was able to excite in everything by the violent
ebullition of his mixed virtues and failings.   For
failings he had undoubtedly—many of us remember
them ; we are this day considering the effect of
them.   But he had no failings which were not
owing to a noble cause ; to an ardent, generous,
perhaps an immoderate, passion for fame ; a passion
which is the instinct of all great souls.   He wor-

shipped that goddess wheresoever she appeared ; but he paid his particular devotions to her in her favourite habitation, in her chosen temple, the House of Commons. Besides the characters of the individuals that compose our body, it is impossible, Mr. Speaker, not to observe that this House has a collective character of its own. That character too, however imperfect, is not unamiable. Like all great public collections of men, you possess a marked love of virtue, and an abhorrence of vice. But among vices, there is none which the House abhors in the same degree with obstinacy. Obstinacy, Sir, is certainly a great vice ; and in the changeful state of political affairs it is frequently the cause of great mischief. It happens, however, very unfortunately that almost the whole line of the great and masculine virtues—constancy, gravity, magnanimity, fortitude, fidelity, and firmness—are closely allied to this disagreeable quality, of which you have so just an abhorrence ; and, in their excess, all these virtues very easily fall into it. He who paid such a punctilious attention to all your feelings, certainly took care not to shock them by that vice which is the most disgustful to you.

That fear of displeasing those who ought most to be pleased, betrayed him sometimes into the other extreme. He had voted, and, in the year 1765, had been an advocate, for the Stamp Act. Things and the disposition of men's minds were changed.

In short, the Stamp Act began to be no favourite in
this House. He therefore attended at the private
meeting in which the resolutions moved by a right
honourable gentleman were settled—resolutions
leading to the repeal. The next day he voted for
that repeal ; and he would have spoken for it too, if
an illness (not, as was then given out, a political,
but to my knowledge, a very real illness) had not
prevented it.

The very next session, as "the fashion of this
world passeth away," the repeal began to be in as
bad an odour in this House as the Stamp Act had
been in the session before. To conform to the
temper which began to prevail, and to prevail mostly
amongst those most in power, he declared, very
early in the winter, that a revenue must be had out
of America. Instantly he was tied down to his
engagements by some who had no objection to such
experiments, when made at the cost of persons
for whom they had no particular regard. The
whole body of courtiers drove him onward. They
always talked as if the king stood in a sort of
humiliated state, until something of the kind should
be done.

Here this extraordinary man, then Chancellor of
the Exchequer, found himself in great straits. To
please universally was the object of his life ; but to
tax and to please, no more than to love and to be
wise, is not given to men. However, he attempted

it. To render the tax palatable to the partisans of
American revenue, he had a preamble stating the
necessity of such a revenue. To close with the
American distinction, this revenue was external or
port-duty ; but again, to soften it to the other party,
it was a duty of supply. To gratify the colonists, it
was laid on British manufactures ; to satisfy the
merchants of Britain, the duty was trivial, and
(except that on tea, which touched only the devoted
East India Company) on none of the grand objects
of commerce. To counterwork the American contraband, the duty on tea was reduced from a shilling
to threepence. But to secure the favour of those
who would tax America, the scene of collection was
changed, and, with the rest, it was levied in the
colonies. What need I say more? This fine-spun
scheme had the usual fate of all exquisite policy.
But the original plan of the duties, and the mode of
executing that plan, both arose singly and solely
from a love of our applause. He was truly the
child of the House. He never thought, did, or said
anything, but with a view to you. He every day
adapted himself to your disposition, and adjusted
himself before it as at a looking-glass.

He had observed (indeed it could not escape him)
that several persons, infinitely his inferiors in all
respects, had formerly rendered themselves considerable in this House by one method alone. They
were a race of men (I hope in God the species is

extinct) who, when they rose in their place, no man
living could divine, from any known adherence to
parties, to opinions, or to principles, from any order
or system in their politics, or from any sequel or
connection in their ideas, what part they were going
to take in any debate.   It is astonishing how much
this uncertainty, especially at critical times, called
the attention of all parties on such men.   All eyes
were fixed on them, all ears open to hear them ;
each party gaped, and looked alternately for their
vote, almost to the end of their speeches.   While
the House hung in this uncertainty, now the " Hear-
hims " rose from his side—now they rebellowed from
the other ; and that party, to whom they fell at
length from their tremulous and dancing balance,
always received them in a tempest of applause.
The fortune of such men was a temptation too great
to be resisted by one to whom a single whiff of
incense withheld gave much greater pain than he
received delight in the clouds of it, which daily rose
about him from the prodigal superstition of innumerable admirers.   He was a candidate for contradictory
honours ; and his great aim was to make those agree
in admiration of him who never agreed in anything
else.

Hence arose this unfortunate Act, the subject of
this day's debate ; from a disposition which, after
making an American revenue to please one, repealed
it to please others, and again revived it in hopes of

pleasing a third, and of catching something in the ideas of all.

This Revenue Act of 1767 formed the fourth period of American policy. How we have fared since then—what woeful variety of schemes have been adopted ; what enforcing, and what repealing ; what bullying, and what submitting ; what doing, and undoing : what straining, and what relaxing ; what assemblies dissolved for not obeying, and called again without obedience ; what troops sent out to quell resistance, and on meeting that resistance, recalled ; what shiftings, and changings, and jumblings of all kinds of men at home, which left no possibility of order, consistency, vigour, or even so much as a decent unity of colour in any one public measure ;—it is a tedious, irksome task. My duty may call me to open it out some other time ; on a former occasion I tried your temper on a part of it ; for the present I shall forbear.

After all these changes and agitations, your immediate situation upon the question on your paper is at length brought to this. You have an Act of Parliament, stating that "it is expedient to raise a revenue in America." By a partial repeal you annihilated the greatest part of that revenue, which this preamble declares to be so expedient. You have substituted no other in the place of it. A Secretary of State has disclaimed, in the king's name, all thoughts of such a substitution in future.

The principle of this disclaimer goes to what has been left, as well as what has been repealed. The tax which lingers after its companions (under a preamble declaring an American revenue expedient, and for the sole purpose of supporting the theory of that preamble) militates with the assurance authentically conveyed to the colonies, and is an exhaustless source of jealousy and animosity. On this state, which I take to be a fair one—not being able to discern any grounds of honour, advantage, peace, or power, for adhering either to the Act or to the preamble—I shall vote for the question which leads to the repeal of both.

If you do not fall in with this motion, then secure something to fight for, consistent in theory and valuable in practice. If you must employ your strength, employ it to uphold you in some honourable right, or some profitable wrong. If you are apprehensive that the concession recommended to you, though proper, should be a means of drawing on you further but unreasonable claims—why then employ your force in supporting that reasonable concession against those unreasonable demands. You will employ it with more grace, with better effect, and with great probable concurrence of all the quiet and rational people in the provinces, who are now united with, and hurried away by, the violent ; having indeed different dispositions, but a common interest. If you apprehend that on a con-

cession you shall be pushed by metaphysical process
to the extreme lines, and argued out of your whole
authority, my advice is this : when you have recovered
your old, your strong, your tenable position, then
face about—stop short—do nothing more—reason
not at all—oppose the ancient policy and practice
of the empire, as a rampart against the speculations
of innovators on both sides of the question ; and
you will stand on great, manly, and sure ground.
On this solid basis fix your machines, and they will
draw worlds towards you.

Your Ministers, in their own and his Majesty's
name, have already adopted the American distinction of internal and external duties.   It is a distinction, whatever merit it may have, that was originally
moved by the Americans themselves ; and I think
they will acquiesce in it, if they are not pushed with
too much logic and too little sense, in all the consequences.   That is, if external taxation be understood, as they and you understand it, when you
please, to be not a distinction of geography, but of
policy ; that it is a power for regulating trade, and
not for supporting establishments.   The distinction,
which is as nothing with regard to right, is of most
weighty consideration in practice.   Recover your
old ground and your old tranquillity—try it—I am
persuaded the Americans will compromise with you.
When confidence is once restored, the odious and
suspicious *summum jus* will perish of course.   The

spirit of practicability, of moderation, and mutual convenience, will never call in geometrical exactness as the arbitrator of an amicable settlement. Consult and follow your experience. Let not the long story with which I have exercised your patience, prove fruitless to your interests.

For my part, I should choose (if I could have my wish) that the proposition of the honourable gentleman for the repeal could go to America without the attendance of the penal Bills. Alone I could almost answer for its success. I cannot be certain of its reception in the bad company it may keep. In such heterogeneous assortments, the most innocent person will lose the effect of his innocency. Though you should send out this angel of peace, yet you are sending out a destroying angel too ; and what would be the effect of the conflict of these two adverse spirits, or which would predominate in the end, is what I dare not say : whether the lenient measures would cause American passion to subside, or the severe would increase its fury—all this is in the hand of Providence ; yet now, even now, I should confide in the prevailing virtue and efficacious operation of lenity, though working in darkness and in chaos, in the midst of all this unnatural and turbid combination ; I should hope it might produce order and beauty in the end.

Let us, Sir, embrace some system or other before we end this session. Do you mean to tax America,

and to draw a productive revenue from thence? If
you do, speak out ; name, fix, ascertain this revenue,
settle its quantity, define its objects, provide for its
collection, and then fight when you have something
to fight for. If you murder, rob ; if you kill, take
possession ; and do not appear in the character of
madmen as well as assassins, violent, vindictive,
bloody and tyrannical, without an object. But may
better counsels guide you !

Again and again revert to your own principles.
Seek peace and ensue it. Leave America, if she
has taxable matter in her, to tax herself. I am
not here going into the distinctions of rights, nor
attempting to mark their boundaries. I do not
enter into these metaphysical distinctions; I hate
the very sound of them. Leave the Americans as
they anciently stood, and these distinctions, born
of our unhappy contest, will die along with it.
They and we, and their and our ancestors, have
been happy under that system. Let the memory
of all actions, in contradiction to that good old
mode, on both sides be extinguished for ever. Be
content to bind America by laws of trade; you have
always done it. Let this be your reason for binding
their trade. Do not burthen them by taxes ; you
were not used to do so from the beginning. Let
this be your reason for not taxing. These are the
arguments of States and kingdoms. Leave the rest
to the schools; for there only they may be discussed

with safety.   But, if intemperately, unwisely, fatally,
you sophisticate and poison the very source of
government, by urging subtle deductions and consequences odious to those you govern, from the
unlimited and illimitable nature of supreme sovereignty, you will teach them by these means to call
that sovereignty itself in question.   When you drive
him hard, the boar will surely turn upon the hunters.
If that sovereignty and their freedom cannot be
reconciled, which will they take ?   They will cast
your sovereignty in your face.   Nobody will be
argued into slavery.   Sir, let the gentlemen on the
other side call forth all their ability ; let the best
of them get up and tell me what one character of
liberty the Americans have, and what one brand of
slavery they are free from, if they are bound in their
property and industry by all the restraints you can
imagine on commerce, and at the same time are
made pack-horses of every tax you chose to impose,
without the least share in granting them.   When
they bear the burthens of unlimited monopoly, will
you bring them to bear the burthens of unlimited
revenue too ?   The Englishman in America will
feel that this is slavery—that it is legal slavery, will
be no compensation, either to his feelings or his
understanding.

A noble lord, who spoke some time ago, is full of
the fire of ingenuous youth ; and when he has
modelled the ideas of a lively imagination by further

experience, he will be an ornament to his country in
either House. He has said that the Americans
are our children, and how can they revolt against
their parent? He says, that if they are not free in
their present state, England is not free; because
Manchester, and other considerable places, are not
represented. So then, because some towns in
England are not represented, America is to have no
representative at all. They are our children; but
when children ask for bread, we are not to give a
stone. Is it because the natural resistance of things
and the various mutations of time hinder our
government, or any scheme of government, from
being any more than a sort of approximation to the
right—is it therefore that the colonies are to recede
from it infinitely? When this child of ours wishes
to assimilate to its parent, and to reflect with a true
filial resemblance the beauteous countenance of
British liberty, are we to turn to them the shameful
parts of our Constitution? are we to give them
our weakness for their strength? our opprobrium
for their glory? and the slough of slavery, which
we are not able to work off, to serve them for their
freedom?

If this be the case, ask yourselves this question,
Will they be content in such a state of slavery? If
not, look to the consequences. Reflect how you
are to govern a people who think they ought to be
free, and think they are not. Your scheme yields

no revenue ; it yields nothing but discontent, disorder, disobedience; and such is the state of
America, that after wading up to your eyes in blood,
you could only end just where you begun ; that is, to
tax where no revenue is to be found, to—my voice
fails me ; my inclination indeed carries me no farther
—all is confusion beyond it.

Well, Sir, I have recovered a little, and before I
sit down I must say something to another point
with which gentlemen urge us. What is to become
of the Declaratory Act asserting the entireness
of British legislative authority, if we abandon the
practice of taxation ?

For my part, I look upon the rights stated in that
Act exactly in the manner in which I viewed them
on its very first proposition, and which I have often
taken the liberty, with great humility, to lay before
you. I look, I say, on the imperial rights of Great
Britain, and the privileges which the colonists ought
to enjoy under these rights, to be just the most
reconcilable things in the world. The Parliament of
Great Britain sits at the head of her extensive
empire in two capacities : one as the local legislature of this island, providing for all things at home,
immediately, and by no other instrument than the
executive power. The other, and I think her
nobler capacity, is what I call her imperial character ;
in which, as from the throne of heaven, she super-
intends all the several inferior legislatures, and

guides and controls them all, without annihilating
any. As all these provincial legislatures are only
co-ordinate with each other, they ought all to be
subordinate to her; else they can neither preserve
mutual peace, nor hope for mutual justice, nor
effectually afford mutual assistance. It is necessary
to coerce the negligent, to restrain the violent, and to
aid the weak and deficient, by the overruling plenitude of her power. She is never to intrude into the
place of the others, whilst they are equal to the
common ends of their institution. But in order to
enable Parliament to answer all these ends of provi-
dent and beneficent superintendence, her powers
must be boundless. The gentlemen who think the
powers of Parliament limited, may please themselves
to talk of requisitions. But suppose the requisitions
are not obeyed? What! Shall there be no
reserved power in the empire, to supply a deficiency
which may weaken, divide, and dissipate the whole?
We are engaged in war—the Secretary of State calls
upon the colonies to contribute—some would do it,
I think most would cheerfully furnish whatever is
demanded—one or two, suppose, hang back, and,
easing themselves, let the stress of the draft lie on
the others---surely it is proper that some authority
might legally say : " Tax yourselves for the common
supply, or Parliament will do it for you." This
backwardness was, as I am told, actually the case of
Pennsylvania for some short time towards the

beginning of the last war, owing to some internal dissensions in the colony. But whether the fact were so, or otherwise, the case is equally to be provided for by a competent sovereign power. But then this ought to be no ordinary power, nor ever used in the first instance. This is what I meant, when I have said at various times that I consider the power of taxing in Parliament as an instrument of empire, and not as a means of supply.

Such, Sir, is my idea of the Constitution of the British Empire, as distinguished from the Constitution of Britain ; and on these grounds I think subordination and liberty may be sufficiently reconciled through the whole ; whether to serve a refining speculatist, or a factious demagogue, I know not ; but enough surely for the ease and happiness of man.

Sir, whilst we held this happy course, we drew more from the colonies than all the impotent violence of despotism ever could extort from them. We did this abundantly in the last war. It has never been once denied—and what reason have we to imagine that the colonies would not have proceeded in supplying government as liberally, if you had not stepped in and hindered them from contributing, by interrupting the channel in which their liberality flowed with so strong a course ; by attempting to take, instead of being satisfied to receive ? Sir William Temple says, that Holland has loaded itself with ten times the impositions which it revolted from Spain, rather than submit to. He says true. Tyranny is a poor provider. It knows neither how to accumulate, nor how to extract.

I charge therefore to this new and unfortunate system the loss not only of peace, of union, and of commerce, but even of revenue, which its friends are contending for. It is morally certain that we have lost at least a million of free grants since the peace. I think we have lost a great deal more ; and that those who look for a revenue from the provinces, never could have pursued, even in that light, a course more directly repugnant to their purposes.

Now, Sir, I trust I have shown, first on that narrow ground which the honourable gentleman measured, that you are likely to lose nothing by complying with the motion, except what you have lost already. I have shown afterwards, that in time of peace you flourished in commerce, and, when war required it, had sufficient aid from the colonies while you pursued your ancient policy ; that you threw everything into confusion when you made the Stamp Act ; and that you restored everything to peace and order when you repealed it. I have shown that the revival of the system of taxation has produced the very worst effects, and that the partial repeal has produced, not partial good, but universal evil. Let these considerations, founded on facts, not one of which can be denied, bring us back to our reason by the road of our experience.

I cannot, as I have said, answer for mixed measures ; but surely this mixture of lenity would give the whole a better chance of success. When you once regain confidence, the way will be clear before you. Then you may enforce the Act of Navigation when it ought to be enforced. You will yourselves open it where it ought still further to be opened. Proceed in what you do, whatever you do, from policy, and not from rancour. Let us act like men, let us act like statesmen. Let us hold some sort of consistent conduct. It is agreed that a revenue is not to be had in America. If we lose the profit, let us get rid of the odium.

On this business of America, I confess I am serious, even to sadness. I have had but one opinion concerning it since I sat, and before I sat, in Parliament. The noble lord will, as usual, probably attribute the part taken by me and my friends in this business to a desire of getting his places. Let him enjoy this happy and original idea. If I deprived him of it, I should take away most of his wit, and all his argument. But I had rather bear the brunt of all his wit, and indeed blows much heavier, than stand answerable to God for embracing a system that tends to the destruction of some of the very best and fairest of His works. But I know the map of England as well as the noble lord, or as any other person ; and I know that the way I take is not the road to preferment. My excellent and honourable friend under me on the floor has trod that road with great toil for upwards of twenty years together. He is not yet arrived at the noble lord's destination. However, the tracks of my worthy friend are those I have ever wished to follow ; because I know they lead to honour. Long may we tread the same road together ; whoever may accompany us, or whoever may laugh at us on our journey! I honestly and solemnly declare, I have in all seasons adhered to the system of 1766, for no other reason than that I think it lay deep in your truest interests—and that, by limiting the exercise, it fixes on the firmest foundations, a real, consistent, well-grounded authority in Parliament. Until you come back to that system, there will be no peace for England.

THE THIRTEEN RESOLUTIONS.

I HOPE, Sir, that notwithstanding the austerity of the Chair, your good-nature will incline you to some degree of indulgence towards human frailty. You will not think it unnatural that those who have an object depending, which strongly engages their hopes and fears, should be somewhat inclined to superstition. As I came into the House full of anxiety about the event of my motion, I found, to my infinite surprise, that the grand penal Bill, by which we had passed sentence on the trade and sustenance of America, is to be returned to us from the other House. I do confess I could not help looking on this event as a fortunate omen. I look upon it as a sort of providential favour, by which we are put once more in possession of our deliberative capacity upon a business so very questionable in its nature, so very uncertain in its issue. By the return of this Bill, which seemed to have taken its flight for ever, we are at this very instant nearly as free to choose a plan for our American government as we were on the first day of the session. If, Sir, we incline to the side of conciliation, we are not at all embarrassed

D 2

(unless we please to make ourselves so) by any incongrous mixture of coercion and restraint. We are therefore called upon, as it were by a superior warning voice, again to attend to America ; to attend to the whole of it together ; and to review the subject with an unusual degree of care and calmness.

Surely it is an awful subject ; or there is none so on this side of the grave. When I first had the honour of a seat in this House, the affairs of that continent pressed themselves upon us, as the most important and most delicate object of parliamentary attention. My little share in this great deliberation oppressed me. I found myself a partaker in a very high trust ; and having no sort of reason to rely on the strength of my natural abilities for the proper execution of that trust, I was obliged to take more than common pains to instruct myself in everything which relates to our colonies. I was not less under the necessity of forming some fixed ideas concerning the general policy of the British empire. Something of this sort seemed to be indispensable ; in order, amidst so vast a fluctuation of passions and opinions, to concentre my thoughts ; to ballast my conduct ; to preserve me from being blown about by every wind of fashionable doctrine. I really did not think it safe or manly to have fresh principles to seek upon every fresh mail which should arrive from America.

At that period I had the fortune to find myself in perfect concurrence with a large majority in this

House. Bowing under that high authority, and
penetrated with the sharpness and strength of that
early impression, I have continued ever since, without the least deviation, in my original sentiments.
Whether this be owing to an obstinate perseverance
in error, or to a religious adherence to what appears
to me truth and reason, it is in your equity to
judge.

Sir, Parliament having an enlarged view of objects,
made, during this interval, more frequent changes in
their sentiments and their conduct, than could be
justified in a particular person upon the contracted
scale of private information. But though I do not
hazard anything approaching to a censure on the
motives of former Parliaments to all those alterations,
one fact is undoubted—that under them the state of
America has been kept in continual agitation.
Everything administered as remedy to the public
complaint, if it did not produce, was at least followed
by a heightening of the distemper; until, by a
variety of experiments, that important country has
been brought into her present situation; a situation
which I will not miscall, which I dare not name;
which I scarcely know how to comprehend in the
terms of any description.

In this posture, Sir, things stood at the beginning
of the session. About that time, a worthy member
of great parliamentary experience, who, in the year
1766, filled the chair of the American Committee

with much ability, took me aside, and, lamenting
the present aspect of our politics, told me things
were come to such a pass, that our former methods
of proceeding in the House would be no longer
tolerated. That the public tribunal (never too
indulgent to a long and unsuccessful opposition)
would now scrutinize our conduct with unusual
severity. That the very vicissitudes and shiftings of
ministerial measures, instead of convicting their
authors of inconstancy and want of system, would be
taken as an occasion of charging us with a predeter-
mined discontent, which nothing could satisfy ; whilst
we accused every measure of vigour as cruel, and
every proposal of lenity as weak and irresolute.
The public, he said, would not have patience to see
us play the game out with our adversaries : we must
produce our hand. It would be expected that those
who for many years had been active in such affairs
should show that they had formed some clear and
decided idea of the principles of colony government ;
and were capable of drawing out something like a
platform of the ground which might be laid for future
and permanent tranquillity.

I felt the truth of what my honourable friend
represented ; but I felt my situation too. His
application might have been made with far greater
propriety to many other gentlemen. No man was
indeed ever better disposed, or worse qualified, for
such an undertaking, than myself. Though I gave

so far into his opinion, that I immediately threw my thoughts into a sort of parliamentary form, I was by no means equally ready to produce them. It generally argues some degree of natural impotence of mind, or some want of knowledge of the world, to hazard plans of government, except from a seat of authority. Propositions are made, not only ineffectually, but somewhat disreputably, when the minds of men are not properly disposed for their reception ; and for my part, I am not ambitious of ridicule—not absolutely a candidate for disgrace.

Besides, Sir, to speak the plain truth, I have in general no very exalted opinion of the virtue of paper government ; nor of any politics in which the plan is to be wholly separated from the execution. But when I saw that anger and violence prevailed every day more and more, and that things were hastening towards an incurable alienation of our colonies, I confess my caution gave way. I felt this as one of those few moments in which decorum yields to a higher duty. Public calamity is a mighty leveller ; and there are occasions when any, even the slightest, chance of doing good, must be laid hold on, even by the most inconsiderable person.

To restore order and repose to an empire so great and so distracted as ours, is, merely in the attempt, an undertaking that would ennoble the flights of the highest genius, and obtain pardon for the efforts of the meanest understanding. Struggling a good

while with these thoughts, by degrees I felt myself
more firm. I derived, at length, some confidence
from what in other circumstances usually produces
timidity. I grew less anxious, even from the idea of
my own insignificance. For, judging of what you
are by what you ought to be, I persuaded myself
that you would not reject a reasonable proposition,
because it had nothing but its reason to recommend
it. On the other hand, being totally destitute of all
shadow of influence, natural or adventitious, I was
very sure that, if my proposition were futile or
dangerous ; if it were weakly conceived, or im-
properly timed, there was nothing exterior to it, of
power to awe, dazzle, or delude you. You will see
it just at it is, and you will treat it just as it
deserves.

The proposition is peace. Not peace through the
medium of war ; not peace to be hunted through the
labyrinth of intricate and endless negotiations ;
not peace to arise out of universal discord, fomented,
from principle, in all parts of the empire ; not peace
to depend on the juridical determination of perplex-
ing questions, or the precise marking the shadowy
boundaries of a complex government. It is simple
peace ; sought in its natural course and in its
ordinary haunts. It is peace sought in the spirit of
peace, and laid in principles purely pacific. I
propose, by removing the ground of the difference,
and by restoring the former unsuspecting confidence

of the colonies in the mother country, to give permanent satisfaction to your people ; and (far from a
scheme of ruling by discord) to reconcile them to
each other in the same act, and by the bond of the
very same interest which reconciles them to British
government.

My idea is nothing more. Refined policy ever
has been the parent of confusion, and ever will be
so, as long as the world endures. Plain good intention, which is as easily discovered at the first view
as fraud is surely detected at last, is, let me say,
of no mean force in the government of mankind.
Genuine simplicity of heart is a healing and
cementing principle. My plan, therefore, being
formed upon the most simple grounds imaginable,
may disappoint some people when they hear it.
It has nothing to recommend it to the pruriency
of curious ears. There is nothing at all new and
captivating in it. It has nothing of the splendour
of the project which has been lately laid upon
your table by the noble lord in the blue ribbon.
It does not propose to fill your lobby with squab-
bling colony agents, who will require the interpo-
sition of your Mace at every instant to keep the
peace amongst them. It does not institute a
magnificent auction of finance, where captivated
provinces come to general ransom by bidding
against each other until you knock down the
hammer, and determine a proportion of payments

beyond all the powers of algebra to equalize and settle.

The plan which I shall presume to suggest derives, however, one great advantage from the proposition and registry of that noble lord's project. The idea of conciliation is admissible. First, the House, in accepting the resolution moved by the noble lord, has admitted, notwithstanding the menacing front of our Address, notwithstanding our heavy Bill of Pains and Penalties, that we do not think ourselves precluded from all ideas of free grace and bounty.

The House has gone farther : it has declared conciliation admissible, previous to any submission on the part of America. It has even shot a good deal beyond that mark, and has admitted that the complaints of our former mode of exerting the right of taxation were not wholly unfounded. That right thus exerted is allowed to have something reprehensible in it, something unwise, or something grievous, since, in the midst of our heat and resentment, we, of ourselves, have proposed a capital alteration ; and, in order to get rid of what seemed so very exceptionable, have instituted a mode that is altogether new ; one that is, indeed, wholly alien from all the ancient methods and forms of Parliament.

The principle of this proceeding is large enough for my purpose. The means proposed by the noble lord for carrying his ideas into execution, I think, indeed are very indifferently suited to the end ;

and this I shall endeavour to show you before I sit down. But, for the present, I take my ground on the admitted principle. I mean to give peace. Peace implies reconciliation; and, where there has been a material dispute, reconciliation does in a manner always imply concession on the one part or on the other. In this state of things I make no difficulty in affirming that the proposal ought to originate from us. Great and acknowledged force is not impaired, either in effect or in opinion, by an unwillingness to exert itself. The superior power may offer peace with honour and with safety. Such an offer from such a power will be attributed to magnanimity. But the concessions of the weak are the concessions of fear. When such a one is disarmed, he is wholly at the mercy of his superior ; and he loses for ever that time and those chances, which, as they happen to all men, are the strength and resources of all inferior power.

The capital leading questions on which you must this day decide are these two : First, whether you ought to concede ; and secondly, what your concession ought to be. On the first of these questions we have gained (as I have just taken the liberty of observing to you) some ground. But I am sensible that a good deal more is still to be done. Indeed, Sir, to enable us to determine both on the one and the other of these great questions with a firm and precise judgment, I think it may be necessary to consider distinctly the true nature and the peculiar circumstances of the object which we have before us. Because after all our struggle, whether we will or not, we must govern America according to that nature and to those circumstances, and not according to our own imaginations, nor according to abstract ideas of right ; by no means according to mere general theories of government, the resort to which appears to me, in our present situation, no better than arrant trifling. I shall therefore endeavour, with your leave, to lay before you some of the most material of these circumstances in as full and as clear a manner as I am able to state them.

The first thing that we have to consider with regard to the nature of the object, is the number of people in the colonies. I have taken for some years · a good deal of pains on that point. I can by no calculation justify myself in placing the number below two millions of inhabitants of our own European blood and colour, besides at least 500,000 others, who form no inconsiderable part of the strength and opulence of the whole. This, Sir, is, I believe, about the true number. There is no occasion to exaggerate where plain truth is of so much weight and importance. But whether I put the present numbers too high or too low is a matter of little moment. Such is the strength with which population shoots in that part of the world that, state the numbers as high as we will, whilst the dispute continues the exaggeration ends. Whilst we are discussing any given magnitude, they are grown to it. Whilst we spend our time in deliberating on the mode of governing two millions, we shall find we have millions more to manage. Your children do not grow faster from infancy to manhood, than they spread from families to communities, and from villages to nations.

I put this consideration of the present and the growing numbers in the front of our deliberation; because, Sir, this consideration will make it evident to a blunter discernment than yours that no partial, narrow, contracted, pinched, occasional system will be at all suitable to such an object. It will show you that it is not to be considered as one of those *minima* which are out of the eye and consideration of the law; not a paltry excrescence of the State; not a mean dependant, who may be neglected with little damage and provoked with little danger. It will prove that some degree of care and caution is required in the handling such an object; it will show that you ought not, in reason, to trifle with so large a mass of the interests and feelings of the human race. You could at no time do so without guilt; and be assured you will not be able to do it long with impunity.

But the population of this country, the great and growing population, though a very important consideration, will lose much of its weight if not combined with other circumstances. The commerce of your colonies is out of all proportion beyond the numbers of the people. This ground of their commerce indeed has been trod some days ago, and with great ability, by a distinguished person at your bar. This gentleman, after thirty-five years—it is so long since he first appeared at the same place to plead for the commerce of Great Britain—has come again before you to plead the same cause, without any other effect of time than that to the fire of imagination and extent of erudition, which even then marked him as one of the first literary characters of his age, he has added a consummate knowledge in the commercial interest of his country, formed by a long course of enlightened and discriminating experience.

Sir, I should be inexcusable in coming after such a person with any detail, if a great part of the members who now fill the House had not the misfortune to be absent when he appeared at your bar. Besides, Sir, I propose to take the matter at periods of time somewhat different from his. There is, if I mistake not, a point of view from whence if you will look at the subject, it is impossible that it should not make an impression upon you.

I have in my hand two accounts: one a comparative state of the export trade of England to its colonies, as it stood in the year 1704, and as it stood in the year 1772. The other a state of the export trade of this country to its colonies alone, as it stood in 1772, compared with the whole trade of England to all parts of the world (the colonies included) in the year 1704. They are from good vouchers; the latter period from the accounts on your table, the earlier from an original manuscript of Davenant, who first established the Inspector-General's office, which has been even since his time so abundant a source of parliamentary information.

The export trade to the colonies consists of three great branches. The African, which, terminating almost wholly in the colonies, must be put to the account of their commerce; the West Indian; and the North American. All these are so interwoven, that the attempt to separate them would tear to pieces the contexture of the whole; and if not entirely destroy, would very much depreciate the value of all the parts. I therefore consider these three denominations to be, what in effect they are, one trade.

The trade to the colonies, taken on the export side, at the beginning of this century—that is, in the year 1704—stood thus:

Exports to North America and the West
   Indies £483,265
To Africa 86,665
                       £569,930

In the year 1772, which I take as a middle year

between the highest and lowest of those lately laid
on your table, the account was as follows :

To North America and the West Indies	£4,791,734
To Africa	866,398
To which if you add the export trade from Scotland, which had in 1704 no existence	364,000
	£6,022,132

From five hundred and odd thousand it has
grown to six millions.   It has increased no less than
twelvefold.   This is the state of the colony trade,
as compared with itself at these two periods, within
this century; and this is matter for meditation.
But this is not all.   Examine my second account.
See how the export trade to the colonies alone in
1772 stood in the other point of view—that is, as
compared to the whole trade of England in 1704 :

The whole export trade of England, including that to the colonies, in 1704	£6,509,000
Export to the colonies alone, in 1772	6,024,000
Difference	£485,000

The trade with America alone is now within less
than £500,000 of being equal to what this great
commercial nation, England, carried on at the
beginning of this century with the whole world !   If
I had taken the largest year of those on your table,

it would rather have exceeded. But, it will be said, is not this American trade an unnatural protuberance that has drawn the juices from the rest of the body ? The reverse. It is the very food that has nourished every other part into its present magnitude. Our general trade has been greatly augmented, and augmented more or less ; in almost every part to which it ever extended ; but with this material difference, that of the six millions which in the beginning of the century constituted the whole mass of our export commerce, the colony trade was but one-twelfth part ; it is now (as a part of sixteen millions) considerably more than a third of the whole. This is the relative proportion of the importance of the colonies at these two periods ; and all reasoning concerning our mode of treating them must have this proportion as its basis ; or it is a reasoning weak, rotten, and sophistical.

Mr. Speaker, I cannot prevail on myself to hurry over this great consideration. It is good for us to be here. We stand where we have an immense view of what is, and what is past. Clouds, indeed, and darkness rest upon the future. Let us, however, before we descend from this noble eminence, reflect that this growth of our national prosperity has happened within the short period of the life of man. It has happened within sixty-eight years. There are those alive whose memory might touch the two extremities. For instance, my Lord Bathurst might

remember all the stages of the progress. He was
in 1704 of an age at least to be made to comprehend such things.   He was then old enough *acta*
parentum jam legere, et quæ sit poterit cognoscere
virtus.   Suppose, Sir, that the angel of this auspicious
youth, foreseeing the many virtues which made him
one of the most amiable, as he is one of the most
fortunate, men of his age, had opened to him in
vision, that when, in the fourth generation the third
Prince of the House of Brunswick had sat twelve
years on the throne of that nation, which (by the
happy issue of moderate and healing counsels) was
to be made Great Britain, he should see his son,
Lord Chancellor of England, turn back the current
of hereditary dignity to its fountain, and raise him
to a higher rank of peerage, whilst he enriched the
family with a new one ; if amidst these bright and
happy scenes of domestic honour and prosperity,
that angel should have drawn up the curtain, and
unfolded the rising glories of his country, and, whilst
he was gazing with admiration on the then commercial grandeur of England, the genius should
point out to him a little speck, scarcely visible in
the mass of the national interest, a small seminal
principle rather than a formed body, and should tell
him—" Young man, there is America—which at this
day serves for little more than to amuse you with
stories of savage men and uncouth manners ; yet
shall, before you taste of death, show itself equal to

the whole of that commerce which now attracts the
envy of the world. Whatever England has been
growing to by a progressive increase of improvement,
brought in by varieties of people, by succession of
civilizing conquests and civilizing settlements in a
series of seventeen hundred years, you shall see as
much added to her by America in the course of a
single life!" If this state of his country had been
foretold to him, would it not require all the sanguine
credulity of youth, and all the fervid glow of
enthusiasm, to make him believe it? Fortunate
man, he has lived to see it! Fortunate indeed, if he
lives to see nothing that shall vary the prospect, and
cloud the setting of his day!

Excuse me, Sir, if turning from such thoughts I
resume this comparative view once more. You
have seen it on a large scale; look at it on a small
one. I will point out to your attention a particular
instance of it in the single province of Pennsylvania.
In the year 1704, that province called for £11,459
in value of your commodities, native and foreign.
This was the whole. What did it demand in 1772?
Why, nearly fifty times as much; for in that year
the export to Pennsylvania was £507,909, nearly
equal to the export to all the colonies together in
the first period.

I choose, Sir, to enter into these minute and
particular details; because generalities, which in all
other cases are apt to heighten and raise the subject,

have here a tendency to sink it. When we speak of the commerce with our colonies, fiction lags after truth ; invention is unfruitful, and imagination cold and barren.

So far, Sir, as to the importance of the object, in view of its commerce, as concerned in the exports from England. If I were to detail the imports, I could show how many enjoyments they procure which deceive the burthen of life ; how many materials which invigorate the springs of national industry, and extend and animate every part of our foreign and domestic commerce. This would be a curious subject indeed—but I must pre-scribe bounds to myself in a matter so vast and various.

I pass therefore to the colonies in another point of view—their agriculture. This they have prose-cuted with such a spirit, that, besides feeding plen-tifully their own growing multitude, their annual export of grain, comprehending rice, has some years ago exceeded a million in value. Of their last harvest, I am persuaded they will export much more. At the beginning of the century some of these colonies imported corn from the mother country. For some time past, the Old World has been fed from the New. The scarcity which you have felt would have been a desolating famine, if this child of your old age, with a true filial piety, with a Roman charity, had not put the full breast

of its youthful exuberance to the mouth of its exhausted parent.

As to the wealth which the colonies have drawn
from the sea by their fisheries, you had all that
matter fully opened at your bar. You surely
thought those acquisitions of value, for they seemed
even to excite your envy ; and yet the spirit by
which that enterprising employment has been
exercised, ought rather, in my opinion, to have
raised your esteem and admiration. And pray, Sir,
what in the world is equal to it ? Pass by the other
parts, and look at the manner in which the people
of New England have of late carried on the whale
fishery. Whilst we follow them among the
tumbling mountains of ice, and behold them penetrating into the deepest frozen recesses of Hudson's
Bay and Davis Straits ; whilst we are looking for
them beneath the Arctic Circle, we hear that they
have pierced into the opposite region of polar cold,
that they are at the Antipodes, and engaged under
the frozen Serpent of the south. Falkland Island,
which seemed too remote and romantic an object for
the grasp of national ambition, is but a stage and
resting-place in the progress of their victorious industry. Nor is the equinoctial heat more discourag-
ing to them than the accumulated winter of both
the Poles. We know that whilst some of them draw
the line and strike the harpoon on the coast of
Africa, others run the longitude, and pursue their

gigantic game along the coast of Brazil. No sea
but what is vexed by their fisheries. No climate
that is not witness to their toils. Neither the perseverance of Holland, nor the activity of France, nor
the dexterous and firm sagacity of English enterprise, ever carried this most perilous mode of hardy
industry to the extent to which it has been pushed
by this recent people ; a people who are still, as it
were, but in the gristle, and not yet hardened into
the bone of manhood. When I contemplate these
things ; when I know that the colonies in general
owe little or nothing to any care of ours, and that
they are not squeezed into this happy form by the
constraints of watchful and suspicious government,
but that, through a wise and salutary neglect, a
generous nature has been suffered to take her own
way to perfection ; when I reflect upon these effects,
when I see how profitable they have been to us, I
feel all the pride of power sink, and all presumption
in the wisdom of human contrivances melt and die
away within me. My rigour relents. I pardon
something to the spirit of liberty.

I am sensible, Sir, that all which I have asserted
in my detail is admitted in the gross ; but that
quite a different conclusion is drawn from it.
America, gentlemen say, is a noble object. It
is an object well worth fighting for. Certainly it is,
if fighting a people be the best way of gaining them.
Gentlemen in this respect will be led to their choice

of means ·by their complexions and their habits.
Those who understand the military art will of
course have some predilection for it. Those who
wield the thunder of the State may have more confidence in the efficacy of arms. But I confess,
possibly for want of this knowledge, my opinion
is much more in favour of prudent management
than of force ; considering force not as an odious,
but a feeble instrument, for preserving a people
so numerous, so active, so growing, so spirited as
this, in a profitable and subordinate connection
with us.

First, Sir, permit me to observe that the use of
force alone is but temporary. It may subdue for a
moment, but it does not remove the necessity of
subduing again ; and a nation is not governed
which is perpetually to be conquered.

My next objection is its uncertainty. Terror is
not always the effect of force, and an armament is
not a victory. If you do not succeed, you are
without resource ; for, conciliation failing, force
remains ; but, force failing, no further hope of
reconciliation is left. Power and authority are
sometimes bought by kindness ; but they can never
be begged as alms by an impoverished and defeated
violence.

A further objection to force is, that you impair
the object by your very endeavours to preserve it.
The thing you fought for is not the thing which you

recover ; but depreciated, sunk, wasted, and con-
sumed in the contest. Nothing less will content
me than whole America. I do not choose to consume its strength along with our own ; because in
all parts it is the British strength that I consume.
I do not choose to be caught by a foreign enemy at
the end of this exhausting conflict, and still less in
the midst of it. I may escape ; but I can make no
insurance against such an event. Let me add, that
I do not choose wholly to break the American
spirit ; because it is the spirit that has made the
country.

Lastly, we have no sort of experience in favour
of force as an instrument in the rule of our colonies.
Their growth and their utility have been owing to
methods altogether different. Our ancient indulgence has been said to be pursued to a fault. It
may be so. But we know, if feeling is evidence,
that our fault was more tolerable than our attempt
to mend it ; and our sin far more salutary than our
penitence.

These, Sir, are my reasons for not entertaining that
high opinion of untried force, by which many gentlemen, for whose sentiments in other particulars I have
great respect, seem to be so greatly captivated. But
there is still behind a third consideration concerning
this object, which serves to determine my opinion on
the sort of policy which ought to be pursued in the
management of America, even more than its popula-

tion and its commerce, I mean its temper and character.

In this character of the Americans, a love of freedom is the predominating feature which marks and distinguishes the whole ; and as an ardent is always a jealous affection, your colonies become suspicious, restive, and untractable, whenever they see the least attempt to wrest from them by force or shuffle from them by chicane, what they think the only advantage worth living for. This fierce spirit of liberty is stronger in the English colonies probably than in any other people of the earth ; and this from a great variety of powerful causes; which to understand the true temper of their minds, and the direction which this spirit takes, it will not be amiss to lay open somewhat more largely.

First, the people of the colonies are descendants of Englishmen. England, Sir, is a nation which still I hope respects, and formerly adored, her freedom. The colonists emigrated from you when this part of your character was most predominant ; and they took this bias and direction the moment they parted from your hands. They are therefore not only devoted to liberty, but to liberty according to English ideas, and on English principles. Abstract liberty, like other mere abstractions, is not to be found. Liberty inheres in some sensible object ; and every nation has formed to itself some favourite point, which by way of eminence becomes

the criterion of their happiness. It happened, you
know, Sir, that the great contests for freedom in this
country were from the earliest times chiefly upon the
question of taxing. Most of the contests in the
ancient commonwealths turned primarily on the right
of election of magistrates ; or on the balance among
the several orders of the State. The question of
money was not with them so immediate. But in
England it was otherwise. On this point of taxes
the ablest pens and most eloquent tongues have
been exercised ; the greatest spirits have acted and
suffered. In order to give the fullest satisfaction
concerning the importance of this point, it was not
only necessary for those who in argument defended
the excellence of the English Constitution to insist on
this privilege of granting money as a dry point of
fact, and to prove that the right had been acknowledged in ancient parchments and blind usage to
reside in a certain body called a House of Commons.
They went much farther ; they attempted to prove, and
they succeeded, that in theory it ought to be so, from
the particular nature of a House of Commons as an
immediate representative of the people, whether the
old records had delivered this oracle or not. They
took infinite pains to inculcate, as a fundamental
principle, that in all monarchies the people must in
effect themselves, mediately or immediately, possess
the power of granting their own money, or no shadow
of liberty could subsist. The colonies draw from

you, as with their life blood, these ideas and principles. Their love of liberty, as with you, fixed and attached on this specific point of taxing. Liberty might be safe, or might be endangered, in twenty other particulars, without their being much pleased or alarmed. Here they felt its pulse ; and as they found that beat, they thought themselves sick or sound. I do not say whether they were right or wrong in applying your general arguments to their own case. It is not easy indeed to make a monopoly of theorems and corollaries. The fact is, that they did thus apply those general arguments ; and your mode of governing them, whether through lenity or indolence, through wisdom or mistake, confirmed them in the imagination, that they, as well as you, had an interest in these common principles.

They were further confirmed in this pleasing error by the form of their provincial legislative assemblies. Their governments are popular in a high degree ; some are merely popular ; in all, the popular representative is the most weighty ; and this share of the people in their ordinary government never fails to inspire them with lofty sentiments, and with a strong aversion from whatever tends to deprive them of their chief importance.

If anything were wanting to this necessary operation of the form of government, religion would have given it a complete effect. Religion, always a principle of energy, in this new people is no way

worn out or impaired ; and their mode of professing
it is also one main cause of this free spirit. The
people are Protestants ; and of that kind which is the
most adverse to all implicit submission of mind and
opinion. This is a persuasion not only favourable
to liberty, but built upon it. I do not think, Sir,
that the reason of this averseness in the dissenting
churches, from all that looks like absolute government, is so much to be sought in their religious
tenets as in their history. Every one knows that
the Roman Catholic religion is at least coeval with
most of the governments where it prevails ; that it
has generally gone hand in hand with them, and
received great favour and every kind of support from
authority. The Church of England too was formed
from her cradle under the nursing care of regular
government. But the dissenting interests have
sprung up in direct opposition to all the ordinary
powers of the world ; and could justify that opposition only on a strong claim to natural liberty. Their
very existence depended on the powerful and un-
remitted assertion of that claim. All Protestantism,
even the most cold and passive, is a sort of dissent.
But the religion most prevalent in our northern
colonies is a refinement on the principle of resistance ;
it is the dissidence of dissent, and the Protestantism
of the Protestant religion. This religion, under a
variety of denominations agreeing in nothing but in
the communion of the spirit of liberty, is predomi-

nant in most of the northern provinces, where the
Church of England, notwithstanding its legal rights,
is in reality no more than a sort of private sect, not
composing most probably the tenth of the people.
The colonists left England when this spirit was high,
and in the emigrants was the highest of all, and
even that stream of foreigners, which has been constantly flowing into these colonies, has, for the
greatest part, been composed of dissenters from the
establishments of their several countries, and have
brought with them a temper and character far from
alien to that of the people with whom they mixed.

Sir, I can perceive by their manner, that some
gentlemen object to the latitude of this description,
because in the southern colonies the Church of
England forms a large body, and has a regular
establishment. It is certainly true. There is, however, a circumstance attending these colonies, which,
in my opinion, fully counterbalances this difference,
and makes the spirit of liberty still more high and
haughty than in those to the northward. It is, that in
Virginia and the Carolinas they have a vast multitude
of slaves. Where this is the case in any part of the
world, those who are free are by far the most proud
and jealous of their freedom. Freedom is to them
not only an enjoyment, but a kind of rank and
privilege. Not seeing there, that freedom, as in
countries where it is a common blessing, and as
broad and general as the air, may be united with

much abject toil, with great misery, with all the
exterior of servitude, liberty looks, amongst them,
like something that is more noble and liberal.   I
do not mean, Sir, to commend the superior morality
of this sentiment, which has at least as much pride
as virtue in it ; but I cannot alter the nature of
man.   The fact is so ; and these people of the
southern colonies are much more strongly, and with
a higher and more stubborn spirit, attached to
liberty, than those to the northward.   Such were
all the ancient commonwealths ; such were our
Gothic ancestors ; such in our days were the Poles ;
and such will be all masters of slaves who are not
slaves themselves.   In such a people, the haughti-
ness of domination combines with the spirit of
freedom, fortifies it, and renders it invincible.

Permit me, Sir, to add another circumstance in
our colonies, which contributes no mean part towards
the growth and effect of this untractable spirit.   I
mean their education.   In no country perhaps in
the world is the law so general a study.   The profession itself is numerous and powerful ; and in most
provinces it takes the lead.   The greater number of
the deputies sent to the Congress were lawyers.   But
all who read (and most do read), endeavour to
obtain some smattering in that science.   I have
been told by an eminent bookseller, that in no
branch of his business, after tracts of popular
devotion, were so many books as those on the law

exported to the plantations. The colonists have now fallen into the way of printing them for their own use. I hear that they have sold nearly as many of Blackstone's Commentaries in America as in England. General Gage marks out this disposition very particularly in a letter on your table. He states that all the people in his Government are lawyers, or smatterers in law; and that in Boston they have been enabled, by successful chicane, wholly to evade many parts of one of your capital penal constitutions. The smartness of debate will say that this knowledge ought to teach them more clearly the rights of legislature, their obligations to obedience, and the penalties of rebellion. All this is mighty well. But my honourable and learned friend on the floor, who condescends to mark what I say for animadversion, will disdain that ground. He has heard, as well as I, that when great honours and great emoluments do not win over this knowledge to the service of the State, it is a formidable adversary to Government. If the spirit be not tamed and broken by these happy methods, it is stubborn and litigious. *Abeunt studia in mores.* This study renders men acute, inquisitive, dexterous, prompt in attack, ready in defence, full of resources. In other countries, the people, more simple, and of a less mercurial cast, judge of an ill principle in government only by an actual grievance; here they anticipate the evil, and judge of the pressure of the

grievance by the badness of the principle. They
augur misgovernment at a distance ; and snuff the
approach of tyranny in every tainted breeze.

The last cause of this disobedient spirit in the
colonies is hardly less powerful than the rest, as it is
not merely moral, but laid deep in the natural constitution of things. Three thousand miles of ocean
lie between you and them. No contrivance can prevent the effect of this distance in weakening government. Seas roll, and months pass, between the order
and the execution ; and the want of a speedy
explanation of a single point is enough to defeat a
whole system. You have, indeed, " winged ministers
of vengeance," who carry your bolts in their pounces
to the remotest verge of the sea. But there a power
steps in, that limits the arrogance of raging passions
and furious elements, and says, " So far shalt thou
go, and no farther." Who are you, that you should
fret and rage, and bite the chains of Nature ?—nothing worse happens to you than does to all nations
who have extensive empire ; and it happens in all.
the forms into which empire can be thrown. In
large bodies, the circulation of power must be less
vigorous at the extremities. Nature has said it.
The Turk cannot govern Egypt, and Arabia, and
Kurdistan, as he governs Thrace ; nor has he the
same dominion in Crimea and Algiers which he has
at Brusa and Smyrna. Despotism itself is obliged
to truck and huckster. The Sultan gets such

obedience as he can. He governs with a loose rein,
that he may govern at all ; and the whole of the
force and vigour of his authority in his centre is
derived from a prudent relaxation in all his borders.
Spain, in her provinces, is perhaps not so well
obeyed as you are in yours. She complies too ; she
submits ; she watches times. This is the immutable
condition, the eternal law, of extensive and detached
empire.

Then, Sir, from these six capital sources ; of
descent ; of form of government ; of religion in the
northern provinces ; of manners in the southern ; of
education ; of the remoteness of situation from the
first mover of government ; from all these causes a
fierce spirit of liberty has grown up. It has grown
with the growth of the people in your colonies, and
increased with the increase of their wealth ; a spirit,
that unhappily meeting with an exercise of power in
England, which, however lawful, is not reconcilable
to any ideas of liberty, much less with theirs, has
kindled this flame that is ready to consume us.

I do not mean to commend either the spirit in
this excess, or the moral causes which produce it.
Perhaps a more smooth and accommodating spirit of
freedom in them would be more acceptable to
us. Perhaps ideas of liberty might be desired
more reconcilable with an arbitrary and boundless
authority. Perhaps we might wish the colonists to
be persuaded that their liberty is more secure when

E

held in trust for them by us (as their guardians
during a perpetual minority) than with any part of it
in their own hands. The question is, not whether
their spirit deserves praise or blame, but what, in
the name of God, shall we do with it? You have
before you the object, such as it is, with all its
glories, with all its imperfections on its head. You
see the magnitude, the importance, the temper, the
habits, the disorders. By all these considerations
we are strongly urged to determine something concerning it. We are called upon to fix some rule
and line for our future conduct, which may give a
little stability to our politics, and prevent the return
of such unhappy deliberations as the present.
Every such return will bring the matter before us in
a still more untractable form. For, what astonishing and incredible things have we not seen already!
What monsters have not been generated from this
unnatural contention! Whilst every principle of
authority and resistance has been pushed, upon both
sides, as far as it would go, there is nothing so solid
and certain, either in reasoning or in practice, that
has not been shaken. Until very lately, all authority in America seemed to be nothing but an
emanation from yours. Even the popular part of
the colony constitution derived all its activity, and
its first vital movement, from the pleasure of the
Crown. We thought, Sir, that the utmost which
the discontented colonists could do was to disturb

authority ; we never dreamt they could of themselves
supply it; knowing in general what an operose
business it is to establish a government absolutely
new.   But having, for our purposes in this contention, resolved that none but an obedient assembly
should sit ; the humours of the people there finding
all passage through the legal channel stopped, with
great violence broke out another way.   Some
provinces have tried their experiment, as we have
tried ours ; and theirs has succeeded.   They have
formed a government sufficient for its purposes,
without the bustle of a revolution, or the troublesome
formality of an election.   Evident necessity and
tacit consent have done the business in an instant.
So well they have done it, that Lord Dunmore—the
account is among the fragments on your table—tells
you that the new institution is infinitely better
obeyed than the ancient government ever was in its
most fortunate periods.   Obedience is what makes
government, and not the names by which it is
called ; not the name of governor, as formerly, or
committee, as at present.   This new government
has originated directly from the people ; and was
not transmitted through any of the ordinary artificial
media of a positive constitution.   It was not a
manufacture ready formed, and transmitted to them
in that condition from England.   The evil arising
from hence is this, that the colonists having once
found the possibility of enjoying the advantages of

order in the midst of a struggle for liberty, such struggles will not henceforward seem so terrible to the settled and sober part of mankind as they had appeared before the trial.

Pursuing the same plan of punishing by the denial of the exercise of government to still greater lengths, we wholly abrogated the ancient government of Massachusetts. We were confident that the first feeling, if not the very prospect of anarchy, would instantly enforce a complete submission. The experiment was tried. A new, strange, unexpected phase of things appeared. Anarchy is found tolerable. A vast province has now subsisted, and subsisted in a considerable degree of health and vigour, for near a twelvemonth, without governor, without public council, without judges, without executive magistrates. How long it will continue in this state, or what may arise out of this unheard-of situation, how can the wisest of us conjecture? Our late experience has taught us that many of those fundamental principles formerly believed infallible, are either not of the importance they were imagined to be ; or that we have not at all adverted to some other far more important and far more powerful principles, which entirely overrule those we had considered as omnipotent. I am much against any further experiments, which tend to put to the proof any more of these allowed opinions, which contribute so much to the public tranquillity. In

effect, we suffer as much at home by this loosening
of all ties, and this concussion of all established
opinions, as we do abroad. For, in order to prove
that the Americans have no right to their liberties, we
are every day endeavouring to subvert the maxims
which preserve the whole spirit of our own. To
prove that the Americans ought not to be free, we
are obliged to depreciate the value of freedom itself;
and we never seem to gain a paltry advantage over
them in debate, without attacking some of those
principles, or deriding some of those feelings, for
which our ancestors have shed their blood.

But, Sir, in wishing to put an end to pernicious
experiments, I do not mean to preclude the fullest
inquiry. Far from it. Far from deciding on a
sudden or partial view, I would patiently go round
and round the subject, and survey it minutely in
every possible aspect. Sir, if I were capable of
engaging you to an equal attention, I would state
that, as far as I am capable of discerning, there are
but three ways of proceeding relative to this stubborn
spirit, which prevails in your colonies, and disturbs
your government. These are: to change that
spirit, as inconvenient, by removing the causes;
to prosecute it as criminal; or, to comply with it
as necessary. I would not be guilty of an imperfect enumeration; I can think of but these three.
Another has indeed been started, that of giving up
the colonies; but it met so slight a reception, that I

do not think myself obliged to dwell a great while upon it. It is nothing but a little sally of anger, like the frowardness of peevish children, who, when they cannot get all they would have, are resolved to take nothing.

The first of these plans, to change the spirit as inconvenient, by removing the causes, I think is the most like a systematic proceeding. It is radical in its principle ; but it is attended with great difficulties, some of them little short, as I conceive, of impossibilities. This will appear by examining into the plans which have been proposed.

As the growing population in the colonies is evidently one cause of their resistance, it was last session mentioned in both Houses, by men of weight, and received not without applause, that in order to check this evil, it would be proper for the Crown to make no further grants of land. But to this scheme there are two objections. The first, that there is already so much unsettled land in private hands as to afford room for an immense future population, although the Crown not only withheld its grants, but annihilated its soil. If this be the case, then the only effect of this avarice of desolation, this hoarding of a royal wilderness, would be to raise the value of the possessions in the hands of the great private monopolists, without any adequate check to the growing and alarming mischief of population.

But if you stopped your grants, what would be

the consequence? The people would occupy without grants. They have already so occupied in many
places. You cannot station garrisons in every part
of these deserts. If you drive the people from one
place, they will carry on their annual tillage, and
remove with their flocks and herds to another. Many
of the people in the back settlements are already little
attached to particular situations. Already they
have topped the Apalachian mountains. From
thence they behold before them an immense plain,
one vast, rich, level meadow; a square of five
hundred miles. Over this they would wander
without a possibility of restraint; they would change
their manners with the habits of their life; would
soon forget a government by which they were
disowned; would become hordes of English Tartars;
and pouring down upon your unfortified frontiers a
fierce and irresistible cavalry, become masters of
your governors and your counsellors, your collectors
and comptrollers, and of all the slaves that adhered
to them. Such would, and in no long time must, be
the effect of attempting to forbid as a crime, and to
suppress as an evil, the command and blessing of
Providence, "Increase and multiply." Such would
be the happy result of an endeavour to keep, as a lair
of wild beasts, that earth which God, by an express
charter, has given to the children of men. Far
different, and surely much wiser, has been our
policy hitherto. Hitherto we have invited our

people, by every kind of bounty, to fixed establishments. We have invited the husbandman to look
to authority for his title. We have taught him
piously to believe in the mysterious virtue of wax
and parchment. We have thrown each tract of land,
as it was peopled, into districts, that the ruling
power should never be wholly out of sight. We
have settled all we could; and we have carefully
attended every settlement with government.

Adhering, Sir, as I do, to this policy, as well as
for the reasons I have just given, I think this new
project of hedging-in population to be neither prudent nor practicable.

To impoverish the colonies in general, and in
particular to arrest the noble course of their marine
enterprises, would be a more easy task. I freely
confess it. We have shown a disposition to a system
of this kind; a disposition even to continue the
restraint after the offence; looking on ourselves as
rivals to our colonies, and persuaded that of course
we must gain all that they shall lose. Much mischief we may certainly do. The power inadequate
to all other things is often more than sufficient for
this. I do not look on the direct and immediate
power of the colonies to resist our violence as very
formidable. In this, however, I may be mistaken.
But when I consider that we have colonies for no
purpose but to be serviceable to us, it seems to my
poor understanding a little preposterous to make

them unserviceable, in order to keep them obedient. It is, in truth, nothing more than the old, and, as I thought, exploded problem of tyranny, which proposes to beggar its subjects into submission. But remember, when you have completed your system of impoverishment, that Nature still proceeds in her ordinary course ; that discontent will increase with misery ; and that there are critical moments in the fortune of all States, when they who are too weak to contribute to your prosperity may be strong enough to complete your ruin. *Spoliatis arma supersunt.*

The temper and character which prevail in our colonies, are, I am afraid, unalterable by any human art. We cannot, I fear, falsify the pedigree of this fierce people, and persuade them that they are not sprung from a nation in whose veins the blood of freedom circulates. The language in which they would hear you tell them this tale would detect the imposition : your speech would betray you. An Englishman is the unfittest person on earth to argue another Englishman into slavery.

I think it is nearly as little in our power to change their republican religion as their free descent; or to substitute the Roman Catholic, as a penalty ; or the Church of England, as an improvement. The mode of inquisition and dragooning is going out of fashion in the Old World, and I should not confide much to their efficacy in the New. The education of the Americans is also on the same unalterable bottom with their religion. You cannot persuade them to burn their books of curious science; to banish their lawyers from their courts of laws; or to quench the lights of their assemblies, by refusing to choose those persons who are best read in their privileges. It would be no less impracticable to think of wholly annihilating the popular assemblies, in which these lawyers sit. The army, by which we must govern in their place, would be far more chargeable to us; not quite so effectual; and perhaps, in the end, full as difficult to be kept in obedience.

With regard to the high aristocratic spirit of Virginia and the southern colonies, it has been proposed, I know, to reduce it, by declaring a general enfranchisement of their slaves. This project has had its advocates and panegyrists; yet I never could argue myself into any opinion of it. Slaves are often much attached to their masters. A general wild offer of liberty would not always be accepted. History furnishes few instances of it. It is sometimes as hard to persuade slaves to be free, as it is to compel freemen to be slaves; and in this auspicious scheme we should have both these pleasing tasks on our hands at once. But when we talk of enfranchisement, do we not perceive that the American master may enfranchise too, and arm servile hands in defence of freedom? A measure to which other people have had recourse more than once, and not without success, in a desperate situation of their affairs.

Slaves as these unfortunate black people are, and dull as all men are from slavery, must they not a little suspect the offer of freedom from that very nation which has sold them to their present masters? from that nation, one of whose causes of quarrel with those masters is their refusal to deal any more in that inhuman traffic. An offer of freedom from England would come rather oddly, shipped to them in an African vessel, which is refused an entry into the ports of Virginia or Carolina, with a cargo of three hundred Angola negroes. It would be curious to see the Guinea captain attempting at the same instant to publish his proclamation of liberty, and to advertise his sale of slaves.

But let us suppose all these moral difficulties got over. The ocean remains. You cannot pump this dry; and as long as it continues in its present bed, so long all the causes which weaken authority by distance will continue. " Ye gods, annihilate but space and time, and make two lovers happy!" was a pious and passionate prayer; but just as reasonable as many of the serious wishes of very grave and solemn politicians.

If then, Sir, it seems almost desperate to think of any alterative course, for changing the moral causes (and not quite easy to remove the natural) which

produce prejudices irreconcilable to the late exercise
of our authority, but that the spirit infallibly will
continue ; and, continuing, will produce such effects
as now embarrass us ; the second mode under consideration is to prosecute that spirit in its overt acts
as criminal.

At this proposition I must pause a moment. The
thing seems a great deal too big for my ideas of
jurisprudence. It should seem to my way of con-
ceiving such matters, that there is a very wide
difference in reason and policy between the mode of
proceeding on the irregular conduct of scattered
individuals, or even of bands of men, who disturb
order within the State, and the civil dissensions
which may, from time to time, on great questions,
agitate the several communities which compose a
great empire. It looks to me to be narrow and
pedantic to apply the ordinary ideas of criminal
justice to this great public contest. I do not know
the method of drawing up an indictment against a
whole people. I cannot insult and ridicule the
feelings of millions of my fellow-creatures, as Sir
Edward Coke insulted one excellent individual (Sir
Walter Raleigh) at the bar. I hope I am not ripe
to pass sentence on the gravest public bodies,
entrusted with magistracies of great authority and
dignity, and charged with the safety of their fellow-
citizens, upon the very same title that I am. I
really think that, for wise men, this is not judicious ;

for sober men, not decent ; for minds tinctured with
humanity, not mild and merciful.

Perhaps, Sir, I am mistaken in my idea of an
empire, as distinguished from a single State or kingdom. But my idea of it is this : that an empire is
the aggregate of many States under one common
head ; whether this head be a monarch, or a pre-
siding republic. It does, in such constitutions, frequently happen (and nothing but the dismal, cold,
dead uniformity of servitude can prevent its happen-
ing) that the subordinate parts have many local
privileges and immunities. Between these privileges
and the supreme common authority the line may be
extremely nice. Of course, disputes, often, too, very
bitter disputes, and much ill blood, will arise. But
though every privilege is an exemption (in the case)
from the ordinary exercise of the supreme authority,
it is no denial of it. The claim of a privilege seems
rather, *ex vi termina*, to imply a superior power. For
to talk of the privileges of a State, or of a person,
who has no superior, is hardly any better than speaking nonsense. Now, in such unfortunate quarrels
among the component parts of a great political
union of communities, I can scarcely conceive anything more completely imprudent than for the head
of the empire to insist that, if any privilege is
pleaded against his will, or his acts, his whole
authority is denied ; instantly to proclaim rebellion,
to beat to arms, and to put the offending provinces

under the ban.   Will not this, Sir, very soon teach
the provinces to make no distinctions on their part?
Will it not teach them that the Government, against
which a claim of liberty is tantamount to high treason,
is a Government to which submission is equivalent to
slavery?   It may not always be quite convenient to
impress dependent communities with such an idea.

We are indeed, in all disputes with the colonies,
by the necessity of things, the judge.   It is true,
Sir.   But I confess that the character of judge in
my own cause is a thing that frightens me.   Instead
of filling me with pride, I am exceedingly humbled
by it.   I cannot proceed with a stern, assured,
judicial confidence, until I find myself in something
more like a judicial character.   I must have these
hesitations as long as I am compelled to recollect
that, in my little reading upon such contests as these,
the sense of mankind has, at least, as often decided
against the superior as the subordinate power.   Sir,
let me add too, that the opinion of my having some
abstract right in my favour would not put me much
at my ease in passing sentence, unless I could be
sure that there were no rights which, in their
exercise under certain circumstances, were not the
most odious of all wrongs, and the most vexatious
of all injustice.   Sir, these considerations have great
weight with me, when I find things so circumstanced,
that I see the same party at once a civil litigant
against me in point of right; and a culprit before

me, while I sit as a criminal judge on acts of his, whose moral quality is to be decided upon the merits of that very litigation. Men are every now and then put, by the complexity of human affairs, into strange situations ; but justice is the same, let the judge be in what situation he will.

There is, Sir, also a circumstance which convinces me that this mode of criminal proceeding is not (at least in the present stage of our contest) altogether expedient ; which is nothing less than the conduct of those very persons who have seemed to adopt that mode, by lately declaring a rebellion in Massachusetts Bay, as they had formerly addressed to have traitors brought hither, under an Act of Henry the Eighth, for trial. For though rebellion is declared, it is not proceeded against as such ; nor have any steps been taken towards the apprehension or conviction of any individual offender, either on our late or our former Address ; but modes of public coercion have been adopted, and such as have much more resemblance to a sort of qualified hostility towards an independent power than the punishment of rebellious subjects. All this seems rather inconsistent ; but it shows how difficult it is to apply these juridical ideas to our present case.

In this situation, let us seriously and coolly ponder. What is it we have got by all our menaces, which have been many and ferocious ? What advantage have we derived from the penal laws we have passed, and which, for the time, have been severe and numerous ?   What advances have we made towards our object, by the sending of a force which, by land and sea, is no contemptible strength ? Has the disorder abated ?   Nothing less.   When I see things in this situation, after such confident hopes, bold promises, and active exertions, I cannot for my life avoid a suspicion that the plan itself is not correctly right.

If then the removal of the causes of this spirit of American liberty be, for the greater part, or rather entirely, impracticable ; if the ideas of criminal process be inapplicable, or if applicable, are in the highest degree inexpedient ; what way yet remains ? No way is open but the third and last—to comply with the American spirit as necessary ; or, if you please, to submit to it as a necessary evil.

If we adopt this mode ; if we mean to conciliate and concede ; let us see of what nature the concession ought to be : to ascertain the nature of our concession we must look at their complaint.   The colonies complain that they have not the characteristic mark and seal of British freedom.   They complain that they are taxed in a Parliament in which they are not represented.   If you mean to satisfy them at all, you must satisfy them with regard to this complaint. If you mean to please any people, you must give them the boon which they ask ; not what you may think better for them, but of a kind totally different·

Such an act may be a wise regulation, but it is no concession ; whereas our present theme is the mode of giving satisfaction.

Sir, I think you must perceive that I am resolved this day to have nothing at all to do with the question of the right of taxation. Some gentlemen startle—but it is true; I put it totally out of the question. It is less than nothing in my consideration. I do not indeed wonder, nor will you, Sir, that gentlemen of profound learning are fond of displaying it on this profound subject. But my consideration is narrow, confined, and wholly limited to the policy of the question. I do not examine whether the giving away a man's money be a power excepted and reserved out of the general trust of government; and how far all mankind, in all forms of polity, are entitled to an exercise of that right by the charter of Nature. Or whether, on the contrary, a right of taxation is necessarily involved in the general principle of legislation, and inseparable from the ordinary supreme power. These are deep questions, where great names militate against each other ; where reason is perplexed ; and an appeal to authorities only thickens the confusion. For high and reverend authorities lift up their heads on both sides ; and there is no sure footing in the middle. This point "is the great Serbonian bog, betwixt Damiata and Mount Casius old, where armies whole have sunk." I do not intend to be overwhelmed in that bog, though in such respectable company. The question with me is, not whether you have a right to render your people miserable, but whether it is not your interest to make them happy. It is not what a lawyer tells me I may do, but what humanity, reason, and justice tell me I ought to do. Is a politic act the worse for being a generous one? Is no concession proper, but that which is made from your want of right to keep what you grant? Or does it lessen the grace or dignity of relaxing in the exercise of an odious claim, because you have your evidence-room full of titles, and your magazines stuffed with arms to enforce them? What signify all those titles and all those arms? Of what avail are they, when the reason of the thing tells me that the assertion of my title is the loss of my suit; and that I could do nothing but wound myself by the use of my own weapons?

Such is steadfastly my opinion of the absolute necessity of keeping up the concord of this empire by a unity of spirit, though in a diversity of operations, that, if I were sure the colonists had, at their leaving this country, sealed a regular compact of servitude; that they had solemnly abjured all the rights of citizens; that they had made a vow to renounce all ideas of liberty for them and their posterity to all generations; yet I should hold myself obliged to conform to the temper I found universally prevalent in my own day, and to govern two millions of men, impatient of servitude, on the principles of freedom. I am not determining a point of law ; I am restoring tranquillity ; and the general character and situation of a people must determine what sort of government is fitted for them. That point nothing else can or ought to determine.

My idea, therefore, without considering whether we yield as matter of right, or grant as matter of favour, is to admit the people of our colonies into an interest in the constitution ; and, by recording that admission in the journals of Parliament, to give them as strong an assurance as the nature of the thing will admit, that we mean for ever to adhere to that solemn declaration of systematic indulgence.

Some years ago, the repeal of a Revenue Act, upon its understood principle, might have served to show that we intended an unconditional abatement of the exercise of a taxing power. Such a measure was then sufficient to remove all suspicion, and to give perfect content. But unfortunate events, since that time, may make something further necessary; and not more necessary for the satisfaction of the colonies, than for the dignity and consistency of our own future proceedings.

I have taken a very incorrect measure of the disposition of the House, if this proposal in itself would be received with dislike. I think, Sir, we have few American financiers. But our misfortune is, we are too acute ; we are too exquisite in our conjectures of the future, for men oppressed with such great and present evils. The more moderate among the opposers of parliamentary concession freely confess that they hope no good from taxation ; but they apprehend the colonists have further views ; and if this point were conceded, they would instantly attack the trade laws. These gentlemen are convinced that this was the intention from the beginning ; and the quarrel of the Americans with taxation was no more than a cloak and cover to this design. Such has been the language even of a gentleman of real moderation, and of a natural temper well adjusted to fair and equal government. I am, however, Sir, not a little surprised at this kind of discourse, whenever I hear it ; and I am the more surprised, on account of the arguments which I constantly find in company with it, and which are often urged from the same mouths, and on the same day.

For instance, when we allege that it is against reason to tax a people under so many restraints in trade as the Americans, the noble lord in the blue ribbon shall tell you that the restraints on trade are futile and useless ; of no advantage to us, and of no burthen to those on whom they are imposed ; that the trade to America is not secured by the Acts of Navigation, but by the natural and irresistible advantage of a commercial preference.

Such is the merit of the trade laws in this posture of the debate. But when strong internal circumstances are urged against the taxes ; when the scheme is dissected ; when experience and the nature of things are brought to prove, and do prove, the utter impossibility of obtaining an effective revenue from the colonies ; when these things are pressed, or rather press themselves, so as to drive the advocates of colony taxes to a clear admission of the futility of the scheme ; then, Sir, the sleeping trade laws revive from their trance, and this useless taxation is to be kept sacred, not for its own sake, but as a counter-guard and security of the laws of trade.

Then, Sir, you keep up revenue laws which are mischievous, in order to preserve trade laws that are useless. Such is the wisdom of our plan in both its members. They are separately given up as of no value ; and yet one is always to be defended for the sake of the other. But I cannot agree with the noble lord, nor with the pamphlet from whence he seems to have borrowed these ideas concerning the inutility of the trade laws. For, without idolizing them, I am sure they are still, in many ways, of great use to us ; and in former times they have been of the greatest. They do confine, and they do greatly narrow, the market for the Americans. But my perfect conviction of this does not help me in the least to discern how the revenue laws form any security whatsoever to the commercial regulations ; or that these commercial regulations are the true ground of the quarrel ; or that the giving way, in any one instance of authority, is to lose all that may remain unconceded.

One fact is clear and indisputable. The public and avowed origin of this quarrel was on taxation. This quarrel has indeed brought on new disputes on new questions ; but certainly the least bitter, and the fewest of all, on the trade laws. To judge which of the two be the real, radical cause of quarrel, we have to see whether the commercial dispute did, in order of time, precede the dispute on taxation ? There is not a shadow of evidence for it. Next, to enable us to judge whether at this moment a dislike to the trade laws be the real cause of quarrel, it is absolutely necessary to put the taxes out of the question by a repeal. See how the Americans act in this position, and then you will be able to discern correctly what is the true object of the controversy, or whether any controversy at all will remain. Unless you consent to remove this cause of difference, it is impossible, with decency, to assert that the dispute is not upon what it is avowed to be. And I would, Sir, recommend to your serious consideration, whether it be prudent to form a rule for punishing people, not on their own acts, but on your conjectures. Surely it is preposterous at the very best. It is not justifying your anger by their misconduct; but it is converting your ill-will into their delinquency.

But the colonies will go farther. Alas! alas! when will this speculation against fact and reason end? What will quiet these panic fears which we entertain of the hostile effect of a conciliatory conduct? Is it true that no case can exist in which it is proper for the Sovereign to accede to the desires of his discontented subjects? Is there anything peculiar in this case to make a rule for itself? Is all authority of course lost when it is not pushed to the extreme? Is it a certain maxim, that the fewer causes of dissatisfaction are left by Government, the more the subject will be inclined to resist and rebel?

All these objections being in fact no more than suspicions, conjectures, divinations, formed in defiance of fact and experience, they did not, Sir, discourage me from entertaining the idea of a conciliatory concession, founded on the principles which I have just stated.

In forming a plan for this purpose, I endeavoured to put myself in that frame of mind which was the most natural and the most reasonable, and which was certainly the most probable means of securing me from all error. I set out with a perfect distrust of my own abilities; a total renunciation of every speculation of my own; and with a profound reverence for the wisdom of our ancestors, who have left us the inheritance of so happy a constitution,

and so flourishing an empire, and, what is a thousand
times more valuable, the treasury of the maxims
and principles which formed the one and obtained
the other.

During the reigns of the kings of Spain of the
Austrian family, whenever they were at a loss in the
Spanish councils, it was common for their statesmen
to say that they ought to consult the genius of Philip
the Second.   The genius of Philip the Second might
mislead them ; and the issue of their affairs showed
that they had not chosen the most perfect standard.
But, Sir, I am sure that I shall not be misled, when
in a case of constitutional difficulty I consult the
genius of the English Constitution.   Consulting at
that oracle (it was with all due humility and piety),
I found four capital examples in a similar case
before me ; those of Ireland, Wales, Chester, and
Durham.

Ireland, before the English conquest, though
never governed by a despotic power, had no Parliament.   How far the English Parliament itself was
at that time modelled according to the present form,
is disputed among antiquaries.   But we have all the
reason in the world to be assured that a form of
Parliament such as England then enjoyed, she
instantly communicated to Ireland ; and we are
equally sure that almost every successive improvement in constitutional liberty, as fast as it was made
here, was transmitted thither.   The feudal baronage

and the feudal knighthood, the roots of our primitive
constitution, were early transplanted into that soil ;
and grew and flourished there. Magna Charta, if it
did not give us originally the House of Commons,
gave us at least a House of Commons of weight
and consequence. But your ancestors did not
churlishly sit down alone to the feast of Magna
Charta. Ireland was made immediately a partaker.
This benefit of English laws and liberties, I confess,
was not at first extended to all Ireland. Mark
the consequence. English authority and English
liberties had exactly the same boundaries. Your
standard could never be advanced an inch before
your privileges. Sir John Davis shows beyond a
doubt that the refusal of a general communication
of these rights was the true cause why Ireland was
five hundred years in subduing ; and after the vain
projects of a military government, attempted in the
reign of, Queen Elizabeth, it was soon discovered
that nothing could make that country English, in
civility and allegiance, but your laws and your forms
of legislature. It was not English arms, but the
English Constitution, that conquered Ireland. From
that time, Ireland has ever had a general Parliament,
as she had before a partial Parliament. You changed
the people ; you altered the religion ; but you never
touched the form or the vital substance of free
government in that kingdom. You deposed kings ;
you restored them ; you altered the succession to

theirs, as well as to your own Crown ; but you never
altered their constitution; the principle of which
was respected by usurpation ; restored with the
restoration of monarchy, and established, I trust, for
ever, by the glorious revolution. This has made
Ireland the great and flourishing kingdom that it is ;
and from a disgrace and a burthen intolerable to this
nation, has rendered her a principal part of our
strength and ornament. This country cannot be
said to have ever formally taxed her. The irregular
things done in the confusion of mighty troubles, and
on the hinge of great revolutions, even if all were
done that is said to have been done, form no
example. If they have any effect in argument, they
make an exception to prove the rule. None of your
own liberties could stand a moment if the casual
deviations from them, at such times, were suffered
to be used as proofs of their nullity. By the lucrative amount of such casual breaches in the constitution, judge what the stated and fixed rule of supply
has been in that kingdom. Your Irish pensioners
would starve if they had no other fund to live on
than taxes granted by English authority. Turn
your eyes to those popular grants from whence all
your great supplies are come ; and learn to respect
that only source of public wealth in the British
empire.

My next example is Wales. This country was
said to be reduced by Henry the Third. It was

said more truly to be so by Edward the First. But though then conquered, it was not looked upon as any part of the realm of England. Its old constitution, whatever that might have been, was destroyed ; and no good one was substituted in its place. The care of that tract was put into the hands of Lord Marchers—a form of government of a very singular kind ; a strange heterogeneous monster, something between hostility and government ; perhaps it has a sort of resemblance, according to the modes of those times, to that of commander-in-chief at present, to whom all civil power is granted as secondary. The manners of the Welsh nation followed the genius of the Government ; the people were ferocious, restive, savage, and uncultivated ; sometimes composed, never pacified. Wales, within itself, was in perpetual disorder ; and it kept the frontier of England in perpetual alarm. Benefits from it to the State there were none. Wales was only known to England by incursion and invasion.

Sir, during that state of things, Parliament was not idle. They attempted to subdue the fierce spirit of the Welsh by all sorts of rigorous laws. They prohibited by statute the sending all sorts of arms into Wales, as you prohibit by proclamation (with something more of doubt on the legality) the sending arms to America. They disarmed the Welsh by statute, as you attempted (but still with more question on the legality) to disarm New England by

an instruction. They made an Act to drag offenders
from Wales into England for trial, as you have done
(but with more hardship) with regard to America.
By another Act, where one of the parties was an
Englishman, they ordained that his trial should be
always by English. They made Acts to restrain
trade, as you do; and they prevented the Welsh
from the use of fairs and markets, as you do
the Americans from fisheries and foreign ports.
In short, when the Statute-book was not quite so
much swelled as it is now, you find no less than
fifteen Acts of penal regulation on the subject of
Wales.

Here we rub our hands—a fine body of precedents
for the authority of Parliament and the use of it !—
I admit it fully; and pray add likewise to these
precedents, that all the while Wales rid this kingdom like an *incubus;* that it was an unprofitable
and oppressive burthen; and that an Englishman
travelling in that country could not go six yards from
the high road without being murdered.

The march of the human mind is slow. Sir, it
was not, until after two hundred years, discovered,
that, by an eternal law, Providence had decreed
vexation to violence, and poverty to rapine. Your
ancestors did, however, at length open their eyes to
the ill husbandry of injustice. They found that the
tyranny of a free people could of all tyrannies the
least be endured; and that laws made against a

whole nation were not the most effectual methods of
securing its obedience. Accordingly, in the twenty-
seventh year of Henry the Eighth, the course was
entirely altered. With a preamble stating the entire
and perfect rights of the Crown of England, it gave
to the Welsh all the rights and privileges of English
subjects. A political order was established; the
military power gave way to the civil; the marches
were turned into counties. But that a nation should
have a right to English liberties, and yet no share at
all in the fundamental security of these liberties—
the grant of their own property—seemed a thing so
incongruous, that, eight years after—that is, in the
thirty-fifth of that reign—a complete and not ill-pro-
portioned representation by counties and boroughs
was bestowed upon Wales by Act of Parliament.
From that moment, as by a charm, the tumults sub-
sided, obedience was restored, peace, order, and
civilization followed in the train of liberty. When
the day-star of the English Constitution had arisen in
their hearts, all was harmony within and without—

> —simul alba nautis
> Stella refulsit,
> Defluit saxis agitatus humor;
> Concidunt venti, fugiuntque nubes,
> Et minax (quod sic voluere) ponto
> Unda recumbit.

The very same year the County Palatine of
Chester received the same relief from its oppressions,
and the same remedy to its disorders. Before this

time Chester was little less distempered than Wales.
The inhabitants, without rights themselves, were the
fittest to destroy the rights of others; and from
thence Richard the Second drew the standing army
of archers, with which for a time he oppressed
England. The people of Chester applied to Parliament in a petition penned as I shall read to you:

"To the King our Sovereign Lord, in most
humble wise shewen unto your excellent Majesty
the inhabitants of your Grace's County Palatine
of Chester: (1). That where the said County
Palatine of Chester is and hath been always
hitherto exempt, excluded and separated out and
from your High Court of Parliament, to have
any Knights and Burgesses within the said
Court; by reason whereof the said inhabitants
have hitherto sustained manifold disherisons,
losses, and damages, as well in their lands, goods,
and bodies, as in the good, civil, and politic
governance and maintenance of the commonwealth of their said country: (2). And forasmuch
as the said inhabitants have always hitherto been
bound by the Acts and Statutes made and
ordained by your said Highness, and your most
noble progenitors, by authority of the said Court,
as far forth as other counties, cities, and boroughs
have been, that have had their Knights and
Burgesses within your said Court of Parliament,
and yet have had neither Knight ne Burgess
there for the said County Palatine; the said
inhabitants, for lack thereof, have been oftentimes
.

touched and grieved with Acts and Statutes
made within the said Court, as well derogatory
unto the most ancient jurisdictions, liberties, and
privileges of your said County Palatine, as prejudicial unto the commonwealth, quietness, rest,
and peace of your Grace's most bounden subjects
inhabiting within the same."

What did Parliament with this audacious address?
—Reject it as a libel? Treat it as an affront to
Government? Spurn it as a derogation from the
rights of legislature? Did they toss it over the
table? Did they burn it by the hands of the common
hangman? They took the petition of grievance, all
rugged as it was, without softening or temperament,
unpurged of the original bitterness and indignation of
complaint; they made it the very preamble to their
Act of redress; and consecrated its principle to all
ages in the sanctuary of legislation.

Here is my third example. It was attended with
the success of the two former. Chester, civilized as
well as Wales, has demonstrated that freedom, and
not servitude, is the cure of anarchy; as religion,
and not atheism, is the true remedy for superstition.
Sir, this pattern of Chester was followed in the reign
of Charles the Second with regard to the County
Palatine of Durham, which is my fourth example.
This county had long lain out of the pale of free
legislation. So scrupulously was the example of
Chester followed, that the style of the preamble is

nearly the same with that of the Chester Act ; and,
without affecting the abstract extent of the authority
of Parliament, it recognizes the equity of not suffering
any considerable district, in which the British subjects may act as a body, to be taxed without their
own voice in the grant.

Now, if the doctrines of policy contained in these
preambles, and the force of these examples in the
Acts of Parliaments avail anything, what can be
said against applying them with regard to America?
Are not the people of America as much Englishmen
as the Welsh ?   The preamble of the Act of Henry
the Eighth says the Welsh speak a language no
way resembling that of his Majesty's English subjects.   Are the Americans not as numerous ?   If
we may trust the learned and accurate Judge
Barrington's account of North Wales, and take that
as a standard to measure the rest, there is no
comparison.   The people cannot amount to above
200,000, not a tenth part of the number in the
colonies.   Is America in rebellion ?   Wales was
hardly ever free from it.   Have you attempted to
govern America by penal statutes ?   You made
fifteen for Wales.   But your legislative authority
is perfect with regard to America ; was it less
perfect in Wales, Chester, and Durham ?   But
America is virtually represented.   What ! does the
electric force of virtual representation more easily
pass over the Atlantic than pervade Wales, which

lies in your neighbourhood ; or than Chester and Durham, surrounded by abundance of representation that is actual and palpable ? But, Sir, your ancestors thought this sort of virtual representation, however ample, to be totally insufficient for the freedom of the inhabitants of territories that are so near and comparatively so inconsiderable. How then can I think it sufficient for those which are infinitely greater and infinitely more remote ?

You will now, Sir, perhaps imagine that I am on the point of proposing to you a scheme for a representation of the colonies in Parliament. Perhaps I might be inclined to entertain some such thought ; but a great flood stops me in my course. *Opposuit natura*—I cannot remove the eternal barriers of the creation. The thing, in that mode, I do not know to be possible. As I meddle with no theory, I do not absolutely assert the impracticability of such a representation. But I do not see my way to it ; and those who have been more confident have not been more successful. However, the arm of public benevolence is not shortened, and there are often several means to the same end. What Nature has disjoined in one way, Wisdom may unite in another. When we cannot give the benefit as we would wish, let us not refuse it altogether. If we cannot give the principal, let us find a substitute. But how? Where? What substitute?

Fortunately, I am not obliged for the ways and

F

means of this substitute to tax my own unproductive
invention. I am not even obliged to go to the
rich treasury of the fertile framers of imaginary
commonwealths, not to the Republic of Plato, not
to the Utopia of More, not to the Oceana of
Harrington. It is before me ; it is at my feet ;
and the rude swain treads daily on it with his
clouted shoon. I only wish you to recognize, for
the theory, the ancient constitutional policy of this
kingdom with regard to representation, as that
policy has been declared in Acts of Parliament ;
and, as to the practice, to return to that mode
which a uniform experience has marked out to
you as best, and in which you walked with security,
advantage, and honour until the year 1763.

My resolutions therefore mean to establish the
equity and justice of a taxation of America by
grant, and not by imposition. To mark the legal
competency of the colony Assemblies for the support
of their government in peace, and for public aids
in time of war. To acknowledge that this legal
competency has had a dutiful and beneficial exercise;
and that experience has shown the benefit of their
grants, and the futility of parliamentary taxation
as a method of supply.

These solid truths compose six fundamental
propositions. There are three more resolutions
corollary to these. If you admit the first set, you
can hardly reject the others. But if you admit the

first, I shall be far from solicitous whether you accept or refuse the last. I think these six massive pillars will be of strength sufficient to support the temple of British concord. I have no more doubt than I entertain of my existence, that, if you admitted these, you would command an immediate peace ; and, with but tolerable future management, a lasting obedience in America. I am not arrogant in this confident assurance. The propositions are all mere matters of fact ; and if they are such facts as draw irresistible conclusions even in the stating, this is the power of truth, and not any management of mine.

Sir, I shall open the whole plan to you, together with such observations on the motions as may tend to illustrate them where they may want explanation. The first is a resolution—

> " That the colonies and plantations of Great Britain in North America, consisting of fourteen separate governments, and containing two millions and upwards of free inhabitants, have not had the liberty and privilege of electing and sending any knights and burgesses, or others, to represent them in the High Court of Parliament."

This is a plain matter of fact, necessary to be laid down, and (excepting the description) it is laid down in the language of the Constitution ; it is taken nearly verbatim from Acts of Parliament.

The second is like unto the first—

"That the said colonies and plantations have
been liable to, and bounded by, several subsidies,
payments, rates, and taxes, given and granted
by Parliament, though the said colonies and
plantations have not their knights and burgesses
in the said High Court of Parliament, of their
own election, to represent the condition of their
country ; by lack whereof they have been oftentimes touched and grieved by subsidies given,
granted, and assented to, in the said Court, in a
manner prejudicial to the commonwealth, quietness, rest, and peace of the subjects inhabiting
within the same."

Is this description too hot or too cold, too strong
or too weak ?   Does it arrogate too much to the
supreme Legislature ?   Does it lean too much to the
claims of the people ?   If it runs into any of these
errors, the fault is not mine.   It is the language of
your own ancient Acts of Parliament :

> Non meus hic sermo, sed quæ præcepit Ofelius,
> Rusticus abnormis sapiens.

It is the genuine produce of the ancient, rustic,
manly, home-bred sense of this country—I did not
dare to rub off a particle of the venerable rust that
rather adorns and preserves, than destroys, the metal.
It would be a profanation to touch with a tool the
stones which construct the sacred altar of peace.   I

would not violate with modern polish the ingenuous and noble roughness of these truly constitutional materials. Above all things, I was resolved not to be guilty of tampering—the odious vice of restless and unstable minds. I put my foot in the tracks of our forefathers; where I can neither wander nor stumble. Determining to fix articles of peace, I was resolved not to be wise beyond what was written; I was resolved to use nothing else than the form of sound words; to let others abound in their own sense; and carefully to abstain from all expressions of my own. What the law has said, I say. In all things else I am silent. I have no organ but for her words. This, if it be not ingenious, I am sure is safe.

There are indeed words expressive of grievance in this second resolution, which those who are resolved always to be in the right will deny to contain matter of fact, as applied to the present case; although Parliament thought them true with regard to the counties of Chester and Durham. They will deny that the Americans were ever " touched and grieved " with the taxes. If they consider nothing in taxes but their weight as pecuniary impositions, there might be some pretence for this denial. But men may be sorely touched and deeply grieved in their privileges, as well as in their purses. Men may lose little in property by the Act which takes away all their freedom. When a man is robbed of a trifle on

the highway, it is not the twopence lost that con-
stitutes the capital outrage. This is not confined to
privileges. Even ancient indulgences withdrawn,
without offence on the part of those who enjoyed
such favours, operate as grievances. But were the
Americans then not touched and grieved by the
taxes, in some measure, merely as taxes? If so,
why were they almost all either wholly repealed, or
exceedingly reduced? Were they not touched and
grieved even by the regulating duties of the sixth of
George the Second? Else why were the duties first
reduced to one-third in 1764, and afterwards to a
third of that third in the year 1766? Were they
not touched and grieved by the Stamp Act? I
shall say they were, until that tax is revived. Were
they not touched and grieved by the duties of 1767,
which were likewise repealed, and which Lord
Hillsborough tells you (for the Ministry) were laid
contrary to the true principle of commerce? Is not
the assurance given by that noble person to the
colonies of a resolution to lay no more taxes on
them, an admission that taxes would touch and
grieve them? Is not the resolution of the noble
lord in the blue ribbon, now standing on your
journals, the strongest of all proofs that parliamentary subsidies really touched and grieved them?
Else why all these changes, modifications, repeals,
assurances, and resolutions?

The next proposition is—

"That, from the distance of the said colonies, and from other circumstances, no method hath hitherto been devised for procuring a representation in Parliament for the said colonies."

This is an assertion of a fact. I go no further on the paper ; though, in my private judgment, a useful representation is impossible ; I am sure it is not desired by them ; nor ought it perhaps by us ; but I abstain from opinions.

The fourth resolution is—

"That each of the said colonies hath within itself a body, chosen in part or in the whole by the freemen, freeholders, or other free inhabitants thereof, commonly called the General Assembly, or General Court ; with powers legally to raise, levy, and assess, according to the several usage of such colonies, duties and taxes towards defraying all sorts of public services."

This competence in the colony Assemblies is certain. It is proved by the whole tenor of their Acts of Supply in all the Assemblies, in which the constant style of granting is, "An aid to his Majesty ; " and Acts granting to the Crown have regularly for near a century passed the public offices without dispute. Those who have been pleased paradoxically to deny this right, holding that none but the British Parliament can grant to the Crown, are wished to look to what is done, not only in the colonies, but in Ireland, in one uniform unbroken tenor every session. Sir, I am surprised that this doctrine should come from some of the law servants of the Crown. I say, that if the Crown could be responsible, his Majesty—but certainly the Ministers, and even these law officers themselves, through whose hands the Acts pass, biennially in Ireland, or annually in the colonies, are in a habitual course of committing impeachable offences. What habitual offenders have been all Presidents of the Council, all Secretaries of State, all First Lords of Trade, all Attorneys and all Solicitors General! However, they are safe, as no one impeaches them; and there is no ground of charge against them, except in their own unfounded theories.

The fifth resolution is also a resolution of fact—

> " That the said General Assemblies, General Courts, or other bodies legally qualified as aforesaid, have at sundry times freely granted several large subsidies and public aids for his Majesty's service, according to their abilities, when required thereto by letter from one of his Majesty's principal Secretaries of State ; and that their right to grant the same, and their cheerfulness and sufficiency in the said grants, have been at sundry times acknowledged by Parliament."

To say nothing of their great expenses in the Indian wars, and not to take their exertion in foreign ones, so high as the supplies in the year

1695 ; not to go back to their public contributions in the year 1710 ; I shall begin to travel only where the journals give me light ; resolving to deal in nothing but fact, authenticated by parliamentary record ; and to build myself wholly on that solid basis.

On the 4th of April 1748 a Committee of this House came to the following resolution :

" Resolved,

" That it is the opinion of this Committee, that it is just and reasonable that the several provinces and colonies of Massachusetts Bay, New Hampshire, Connecticut, and Rhode Island, be reimbursed the expenses they have been at in taking and securing to the Crown of Great Britain the island of Cape Breton and its dependencies."

The expenses were immense for such colonies. They were above £200,000 sterling ; money first raised and advanced on their public credit.

On the 28th of January 1756 a message from the king came to us, to this effect :

" His Majesty, being sensible of the zeal and vigour with which his faithful subjects of certain colonies in North America have exerted them-selves in defence of his Majesty's just rights and possessions, recommends it to this House to take the same into their consideration, and to enable his Majesty to give them such assistance as may be a proper reward and encouragement."

On the 3rd of February 1756 the House came
to a suitable resolution, expressed in words nearly
the same as those of the message ; but with the
further addition that the money then voted was as an
encouragement to the colonies to exert themselves
with vigour.   It will not be necessary to go through
all the testimonies which your own records have
given to the truth of my resolutions, I will only
refer you to the places in the journals :

Vol. xxvii.—16th and 19th May 1757.
Vol. xxviii.—June 1st, 1758 ; April 26th and 30th,
          1759 ; March 26th and 31st, and
          April 28th, 1760 ; Jan. 9th and
          20th, 1761.
Vol. xxix.—Jan. 22nd and 26th, 1762 ; March
          14th and 17th, 1763.

Sir, here is the repeated acknowledgment of
Parliament that the colonies not only gave, but gave
to satiety.   This nation has formally acknowledged
two things : first, that the colonies had gone beyond
their abilities, Parliament having thought it necessary
to reimburse them ; secondly, that they had acted
legally and laudably in their grants of money, and
their maintenance of troops, since the compensation
is expressly given as reward and encouragement.
Reward is not bestowed for acts that are unlawful ;
and encouragement is not held out to things that
deserve reprehension.   My resolution therefore does
nothing more than collect into one proposition what

is scattered through your journals. I give you nothing but your own; and you cannot refuse in the gross what you have so often acknowledged in detail. The admission of this, which will be so honourable to them and to you, will indeed be mortal to all the miserable stories, by which the passions of the misguided people have been engaged in an unhappy system. The people heard, indeed, from the beginning of these disputes, one thing continually dinned in their ears, that reason and justice demanded that the Americans, who paid no taxes, should be compelled to contribute. How did that fact of their paying nothing stand, when the taxing system began? When Mr. Grenville began to form his system of American revenue, he stated in this House that the colonies were then in debt two millions six hundred thousand pounds sterling money; and was of opinion they would discharge that debt in four years. On this state, those untaxed people were actually subject to the payment of taxes to the amount of six hundred and fifty thousand a year. In fact, however, Mr. Grenville was mistaken. The funds given for sinking the debt did not prove quite so ample as both the colonies and he expected. The calculation was too sanguine; the reduction was not completed till some years after, and at different times in different colonies. However, the taxes after the war continued too great to bear any addition, with prudence

or propriety; and when the burthens imposed in
consequence of former requisitions were discharged,
our tone became too high to resort again to requisition.   No colony, since that time, ever has had any
requisition whatsoever made to it.

We see the sense of the Crown, and the sense of
Parliament, on the productive nature of a revenue
by grant.   Now, search the same journals for the
produce of the revenue by imposition—where is it?
Let us know the volume and the page.   What is
the gross, what is the net produce?   To what service
is it applied?   How have you appropriated its
surplus?   What, can none of the many skilful
index-makers that we are now employing find any
trace of it?   Well, let them and that rest together.
But are the journals, which say nothing of the
revenue, as silent on the discontent?   Oh no! a
child may find it.   It is the melancholy burthen and
blot of every page.

I think, then, I am, from those journals, justified
in the sixth and last resolution, which is—

> "That it hath been found by experience that
> the manner of granting the said supplies and
> aids by the said General Assemblies, hath been
> more agreeable to the said colonies, and more
> beneficial and conducive to the public service,
> than the mode of giving and granting aids in
> Parliament, to be raised and paid in the said
> colonies."

This makes the whole of the fundamental part of the plan. The conclusion is irresistible. You cannot say that you were driven by any necessity to an exercise of the utmost rights of legislature. You cannot assert that you took on yourselves the task of imposing colony taxes from the want of another legal body that is competent to the purpose of supplying the exigencies of the State without wounding the prejudices of the people. Neither is it true that the body so qualified, and having that competence, had neglected the duty.

The question now, on all this accumulated matter, is—whether you will choose to abide by a profitable experience or a mischievous theory ; whether you choose to build on imagination or fact ; whether you prefer enjoyment or hope ; satisfaction in your subjects, or discontent ?

If these propositions are accepted, everything which has been made to enforce a contrary system must, I take it for granted, fall along with it. On that ground, I have drawn the following resolution, which, when it comes to be moved, will naturally be divided in a proper manner :

" That it may be proper to repeal an Act, made in the seventh year of the reign of his present Majesty, intituled, 'An Act for granting certain duties in the British colonies and plantations in America, for allowing a drawback of the duties of customs upon the exportation from this king-

dom, of coffee and cocoa-nuts of the produce of
the said colonies or plantations ; for discontinu-
ing the drawbacks payable on China earthenware
exported to America ; and for more effectually
preventing the clandestine running of goods in
the said colonies and plantations. And that it may
be proper to repeal an Act, made in the fourteenth year of the reign of his present Majesty,
intituled, An Act to discontinue, in such manner and for such time as are therein mentioned, the landing and discharging, lading or
shipping, of goods, wares, and merchandise, at
the town and within the harbour of Boston, in
the province of Massachusetts Bay, in North
America.   And that it may be proper to repeal
an Act, made in the fourteenth year of the reign
of his present Majesty, intituled, An Act for the
impartial administration of justice, in the cases
of persons questioned for any acts done by them,
in the execution of the law, or for the suppression
of riots and tumults, in the province of Massachusetts Bay, in New England.   And that it
may be proper to repeal an Act, made in the
fourteenth year of the reign of his present
Majesty, intituled, An Act for the better regulating the government of the province of the
Massachusetts Bay, in New England.   And
also, that it may be proper to explain and amend
an Act, made in the thirty-fifth year of the reign
of King Henry the Eighth, intituled, An Act
for the trial of treasons committed out of the
king's dominions."

I wish, Sir, to repeal the Boston Port Bill, because (independently of the dangerous precedent of suspending the rights of the subject during the king's pleasure) it was passed, as I apprehend, with less regularity, and on more partial principles, than it ought. The corporation of Boston was not heard before it was condemned. Other towns, full as guilty as she was, have nót had their ports blocked up. Even the Restraining Bill of the present session dóes not go to the length of the Boston Port Act. The same ideas of prudence, which induced you not to extend equal punishment to equal guilt, even when you were punishing, induced me, who mean not to chastise, but to reconcile, to be satisfied with the punishment already partially inflicted.

Ideas of prudence and accommodation to circumstances prevent you from taking away the charters of Connecticut and Rhode Island, as you have taken away that of Massachusetts colony, though the Crown has far less power in the two former provinces than it enjoyed in the latter ; and though the abuses have been full as great and as flagrant in the exempted as in the punished. The same reasons of prudence and accommodation have weight with me in restoring the charter of Massachusetts Bay. Besides, Sir, the Act which changes the charter of Massachusetts is in many particulars so exceptionable, that if I did not wish absolutely to repeal, I

would by all means desire to alter it; as several of
its provisions tend to the subversion of all public
and private justice. Such, among others, is the
power in the governor to change the sheriff at his
pleasure, and to make a new returning officer for
every special cause. It is shameful to behold such
a regulation standing among English laws.

The Act for bringing persons accused of committing murder under the orders of Government to
England for trial is but temporary. That Act has
calculated the probable duration of our quarrel with
the colonies, and is accommodated to that supposed
duration. I would hasten the happy moment of
reconciliation ; and therefore must, on my principle,
get rid of that most justly obnoxious Act.

The Act of Henry the Eighth, for the trial of
treasons, I do not mean to take away, but to confine it to its proper bounds and original intention ;
to make it expressly for trial of treasons (and the
greatest treasons may be committed) in places
where the jurisdiction of the Crown does not
extend.

Having guarded the privileges of local legislature,
I would next secure to the colonies a fair and
unbiassed judicature ; for which purpose, Sir, I
propose the following resolution :

> " That, from the time when the General Assem-
> bly or General Court of any colony or plantation
> in North America, shall have appointed by Act

of Assembly, duly confirmed, a settled salary to the offices of the Chief Justice and other judges of the Superior Court, it may be proper that the said Chief Justice and other judges of the Superior Courts of such colony, shall hold his and their office and offices during their good behaviour, and shall not be removed therefrom but when the said removal shall be adjudged by his Majesty in Council, upon a hearing on complaint from the General Assembly, or on a complaint from the Governor or Council, or the House of Representatives severally, or of the colony in which the said Chief Justice and other judges have exercised the said offices."

The next resolution relates to the Courts of Admiralty. It is this :

" That it may be proper to regulate the Courts of Admiralty, or Vice-Admiralty, authorized by the fifteenth chapter of the fourth of George the Third, in such a manner as to make the same more commodious to those who sue, or are sued, in the said courts, and to provide for the more decent maintenance of the judges in the same."

These courts I do not wish to take away ; they are in themselves proper establishments. This court is one of the capital securities of the Act of Navigation. The extent of its jurisdiction, indeed, has been increased ; but this is altogether as proper, and is indeed on many accounts more eligible, where new powers were wanted, than a court absolutely new. But courts incommodiously situated, in effect deny justice ; and a court partaking in the fruits of its own condemnation is a robber. The Congress complain, and complain justly, of this grievance.

These are the three consequential propositions. I have thought of two or three more ; but they come rather too near detail, and to the province of executive government ; which I wish Parliament always to superintend, never to assume. If the first six are granted, congruity will carry the latter three. If not, the things that remain unrepealed will be, I hope, rather unseemly incumbrances on the building, than very materially detrimental to its strength and stability.

Here, Sir, I should close ; but I plainly perceive some objections remain, which I ought, if possible, to remove. The first will be, that, in resorting to the doctrine of our ancestors, as contained in the preamble to the Chester Act, I prove too much ; that the grievance from a want of representation, stated in that preamble, goes to the whole of legislation as well as to taxation. And that the colonies, grounding themselves upon that doctrine, will apply it to all parts of legislative authority.

To this objection, with all possible deference and humility, and wishing as little as any man living to impair the smallest particle of our supreme authority, I answer, that the words are the words of Parliament,

and not mine ; and that all false and inconclusive
inferences drawn from them are not mine, for I
heartily disclaim any such inference. I have chosen
the words of an Act of Parliament which Mr. Grenville, surely a tolerably zealous and very judicious
advocate for the sovereignty of Parliament, formerly
moved to have read at your table in confirmation of
his tenets. It is true that Lord Chatham considered
these preambles as declaring strongly in favour of his
opinions. He was a no less powerful advocate for
the privileges of the Americans. Ought I not from
hence to presume that these preambles are as
favourable as possible to both, when properly understood ; favourable both to the rights of Parliament,
and to the privilege of the dependencies of this
Crown ? But, Sir, the object of grievance in my
resolution I have not taken from the Chester, but
from the Durham Act, which confines the hardship
of want of representation to the case of subsidies ;
and which therefore falls in exactly with the case
of the colonies. But whether the unrepresented
counties were *de jure* or *de facto* bound, the
preambles do not accurately distinguish ; nor indeed
was it necessary ; for, whether *de jure* or *de facto*, the
Legislature thought the exercise of the power of
taxing, as of right, or as of fact without right, equally
a grievance, and equally oppressive.

I do not know that the colonies have, in any
general way, or in any cool hour, gone much beyond

the demand of immunity in relation to taxes.   It is
not fair to judge of the temper or dispositions of any
man, or any set of men, when they are composed
and at rest, from their conduct, or their expressions,
in a state of disturbance and irritation.   It is besides
a very great mistake to imagine that mankind follow
up practically any speculative principle, either of
government or of freedom, as far as it will go
in argument and logical illation.   We Englishmen
stop very short of the principles upon which we
support any given part of our Constitution ; or even
the whole of it together.   I could easily, if I had not
already tired you, give you very striking and convincing instances of it.   This is nothing but what is
natural and proper.   All government, indeed every
human benefit and enjoyment, every virtue, and
every prudent act, is founded on compromise and
barter.   We balance inconveniences ; we give and
take ; we remit some rights, that we may enjoy
others ; and we choose rather to be happy citizens,
than subtle disputants.   As we must give away
some natural liberty, to enjoy civil advantages ; so we
must sacrifice some civil liberties, for the advantages
to be derived from the communion and fellowship of
a great empire.   But, in all fair dealings, the thing
bought must bear some proportion to the purchase
paid.   None will barter away the immediate jewel
of his soul.   Though a great house is apt to make
slaves haughty, yet it is purchasing a part of the

artificial importance of a great empire too dear, to
pay for it all essential rights, and all the intrinsic
dignity of human nature.   None of us who would
not risk his life rather than fall under a government
purely arbitrary.   But although there are some
amongst us who think our Constitution wants many
improvements, to make it a complete system of
liberty ; perhaps none who are of that opinion would
think it right to aim at such improvement by dis-
turbing his country and risking everything that is
dear to him.   In every arduous enterprise, we consider what we are to lose, as well as what we are to
gain ; and the more and better stake of liberty every
people possess, the less they will hazard in a vain
attempt to make it more.   These are the cords of
man.   Man acts from adequate motives relative to
his interest ; and not on metaphysical speculations.
Aristotle, the great master of reasoning, cautions us,
and with great weight and propriety, against this
species of delusive geometrical accuracy in moral
arguments, as the most fallacious of all sophistry.

The Americans will have no interest contrary to
the grandeur and glory of England, when they are
not oppressed by the weight of it ; and they will
rather be inclined to respect the acts of a superintending legislature ; when they see them the acts of that
power which is itself the security, not the rival, of
their secondary importance.   In this assurance my
mind most perfectly acquiesces ; and I confess I

feel not the least alarm from the discontents which
are to arise from putting people at their ease ; nor
do I apprehend the destruction of this empire, from
giving, by an act of free grace and indulgence, to
two millions of my fellow-citizens some share of
those rights upon which I have always been taught
to value myself.

It is said, indeed, that this power of granting,
vested in American assemblies, would dissolve the
unity of the empire ; which was preserved entire,
although Wales, and Chester and Durham were
added to it. Truly, Mr. Speaker, I do not know
what this unity means ; nor has it ever been heard
of, that I know, in the constitutional policy of this
country. The very idea of subordination of parts
excludes this notion of simple and undivided unity.
England is the head, but she is not the head and
the members too. Ireland has ever had from the
beginning a separate, but not an independent, legislature, which, far from distracting, promoted the union
of the whole. Everything was sweetly and har-
moniously disposed through both islands for the
conservation of English dominion, and the communication of English liberties. I do not see that
the same principles might not be carried into twenty
islands, and with the same good effect. This is my
model with regard to America, as far as the internal
circumstances of the two countries are the same. I
know no other unity of this empire, than I can

draw from its example during these periods, when it seemed to my poor understanding more united than it is now, or than it is likely to be by the present methods.

But since I speak of these methods, I recollect, Mr. Speaker, almost too late, that I promised, before I finished, to say something of the proposition of the noble lord on the floor, which has been so lately received, and stands on your journals. I must be deeply concerned, whenever it is my misfortune to continue a difference with the majority of this House. But as the reasons for that difference are my apology for thus troubling you, suffer me to state them in a very few words. I shall compress them into as small a body as I possibly can, having already debated that matter at large, when the question was before the committee.

First, then, I cannot admit that proposition of a ransom by auction, because it is a mere project. It is a thing new, unheard of, supported by no experience, justified by no analogy, without example of our ancestors, or root in the Constitution. It is neither regular parliamentary taxation, nor colony grant. *Experimentum in corpore vili*, is a good rule, which will ever make me adverse to any trial of experiments on what is certainly the most valuable of all subjects, the peace of this empire.

Secondly, it is an experiment which must be fatal in the end to our Constitution. For what is it but a scheme for taxing the colonies in the antechamber of the noble lord and his successors? To settle the quotas and proportions in this House is clearly impossible. You, Sir, may flatter yourself you shall sit a State auctioneer, with your hammer in your hand, and knock down to each colony as it bids. But to settle (on the plan laid down by the noble lord) the true proportional payment for four or five and twenty governments, according to the absolute and the relative wealth of each, and according to the British proportion of wealth and burthen, is a wild and chimerical notion. This new taxation must therefore come in by the back door of the Constitution. Each quota must be brought to this House ready formed ; you can neither add nor alter. You must register it. You can do nothing further. For on what grounds can you deliberate either before or after the proposition ? You cannot hear the counsel for all these provinces, quarrelling each on its own quantity of payment, and its proportion to others. If you should attempt it, the committee of provincial ways and means, or by whatever other name it will delight to be called, must swallow up all the time of Parliament.

Thirdly, it does not give satisfaction to the complaint of the colonies. They complain that they are taxed without their consent ; you answer that you will fix the sum at which they shall be taxed. That is, you give them the very grievance for the

remedy. You tell them, indeed, that you will leave
the mode to themselves. I really beg pardon ; it
gives me pain to mention it ; but you must be
sensible that you will not perform this part of the
compact. For, suppose the colonies were to lay the
duties, which furnished their contingent, upon the
importation of your manufactures ; you know you
would never suffer such a tax to be laid. You
know, too, that you would not suffer many other
modes of taxation. So that, when you come to
explain yourself, it will be found that you will
neither leave to themselves the quantum nor the
mode ; nor indeed anything. The whole is delusion
from one end to the other.

Fourthly, this method of ransom by auction,
unless it be universally accepted, will plunge you
into great and inextricable difficulties. In what
year of our Lord are the proportions of payments to
be settled ? To say nothing of the impossibility
that colony agents should have general powers of
taxing the colonies at their discretion ; consider, I
implore you, that the communication by special
messages, and orders between these agents and their
constituents on each variation of the case, when the
parties come to contend together, and to dispute on
their relative proportions, will be a matter of delay,
perplexity, and confusion that never can have
an end.

If all the colonies do not appear at the outcry,

what is the condition of those assemblies who offer,
by themselves or their agents, to tax themselves up
to your ideas of their proportion ?   The refractory
colonies, who refuse all composition, will remain
taxed only to your old impositions, which, however
grievous in principle, are trifling as to production.
The obedient colonies in this scheme are heavily
taxed ; the refractory remain unburthened.   What
will you do ?   Will you lay new and heavier taxes
by Parliament on the disobedient ?   Pray consider in
what way you can do it.   You are perfectly convinced
that, in the way of taxing, you can do nothing but
at the ports.   Now, suppose it is Virginia that
refuses to appear at your auction, while Maryland
and North Carolina bid handsomely for their ransom,
and are taxed to your quota, how will you put these
colonies on a par ?   Will you tax the tobacco of
Virginia ?   If you do, you give its death-wound to
your English revenue at home, and to one of the
very greatest articles of your own foreign trade.   If
you tax the import of that rebellious colony, what
do you tax but your own manufactures, or the goods
of some other obedient and already well-taxed
colony ?   Who has said one word on this labyrinth
of detail, which bewilders you more and more as
you enter into it ?   Who has presented, who can
present you with a clue, to lead you out of it ?   I
think, Sir, it is impossible that you should not
recollect that the colony bounds are so implicated in

one another (you know it by your other experiments
in the Bill for prohibiting the New England fishery),
that you can lay no possible restraints on almost any
of them which may not be presently eluded, if you
do not confound the innocent with the guilty, and
burthen those whom, upon every principle, you ought
to exonerate. He must be grossly ignorant of
America who thinks that, without falling into this
confusion of all rules of equity and policy, you
can restrain any single colony, especially Virginia
and Maryland, the central and most important of
them all.

Let it also be considered that, either in the present confusion you settle a permanent contingent,
which will and must be trifling, and then you have
no effectual revenue ; or you change the quota at
every exigency ; and then on every new repartition
you will have a new quarrel.

Reflect besides, that when you have fixed a quota
for every colony you have not provided for prompt
and punctual payment. Suppose, one, two, five, ten
years' arrears. You cannot issue a Treasury extent
against the failing colony. You must make new
Boston Port Bills, new restraining laws, new Acts
for dragging men to England for trial. You must
send out new fleets, new armies. All is to begin
again. From this day forward the empire is never
to know an hour's tranquillity. An intestine fire will
be kept alive in the bowels of the colonies, which

one time or other must consume this whole empire.
I allow indeed that the empire of Germany raises
her revenue and her troops by quotas and con-
tingents ; but the revenue of the empire, and the
army of the empire, is the worst revenue and the
worst army in the world.

Instead of a standing revenue, you will therefore
have a perpetual quarrel. Indeed, the noble lord
who proposed this project of a ransom by auction
seemed himself to be of that opinion. His project
was rather designed for breaking the union of the
colonies, than for establishing a revenue. He con-
fessed, he apprehended that his proposal would not
be to their taste. I say this scheme of disunion
seems to be at the bottom of the project ; for I will
not suspect that the noble lord meant nothing but
merely to delude the nation by an airy phantom
which he never intended to realize. But whatever
his views may be, as I propose the peace and union
of the colonies as the very foundation of my plan, it
cannot accord with one whose foundation is perpetual discord.

Compare the two. This I offer to give you is
plain and simple. The other full of perplexed and
intricate mazes. This is mild ; that harsh. This
is found by experience effectual for its purposes ; the
other is a new project. This is universal ; the other
calculated for certain colonies only. This is immediate in its conciliatory operation ; the other remote,

contingent, full of hazard. Mine is what becomes the dignity of a ruling people, gratuitous, unconditional, and not held out as a matter of bargain and sale. I have done my duty in proposing it to you. I have indeed tired you by a long discourse ; but this is the misfortune of those to whose influence nothing will be conceded, and who must win every inch of their ground by argument. You have heard me with goodness. May you decide with wisdom ! For my part, I feel my mind greatly disburthened by what I have done to-day. I have been the less fearful of trying your patience, because on this subject I mean to spare it altogether in future. I have this comfort, that in every stage of the American affairs I have steadily opposed the measures that have produced the confusion, and may bring on the destruction, of this empire. I now go so far as to risk a proposal of my own. If I cannot give peace to my country, I give it to my conscience.

But what (says the financier) is peace to us without money ? Your plan gives us no revenue. No ! But it does ; for it secures to the subject the power of *refusal*, the first of all revenues. Experience is a cheat, and fact a liar, if this power in the subject of proportioning his grant, or of not granting at all, has not been found the richest mine of revenue ever discovered by the skill or by the fortune of man. It does not indeed vote you

£152,750 11*s*. 2¾*d*., nor any other paltry limited
sum ; but it gives the strong box itself, the fund,
the bank, from whence only revenues can arise
amongst a people sensible of freedom : *Posita
luditur arca.* Cannot you, in England ; cannot
you, at this time of day ; cannot you, a House of
Commons, trust to the principle which has raised so
mighty a revenue, and accumulated a debt of near
140 millions in this country ? Is this principle to
be true in England, and false everywhere else? Is
it not true in Ireland ? Has it not hitherto been true
in the colonies ? Why should you presume that in
any country a body duly constituted for any function
will neglect to perform its duty, and abdicate its
trust ? Such a presumption would go against all
governments in all modes. But, in truth, this dread
of ·penury of supply, from a free assembly, has no
foundation in Nature. For first observe, that, besides
the desire which all men have naturally of supporting
the honour of their own government, that sense of
dignity, and that security to property, which ever
attends freedom, has a tendency to increase the stock
of the free community. Most may be taken where
most is accumulated. And what is the soil or
climate where experience has not uniformly proved
that the voluntary flow of heaped-up plenty, bursting
from the weight of its own rich luxuriance, has ever
run with a more copious stream of revenue than
could be squeezed from the dry husks of oppressed

indigence by the straining of all the politic machinery in the world ?

Next, we know that parties must ever exist in a free country. We know, too, that the emulations of such parties, their contradictions, their reciprocal necessities, their hopes, and their fears, must send them all in their turns to him that holds the balance of the State. The parties are the gamesters ; but Government keeps the table, and is sure to be the winner in the end. When this game is played, I really think it is more to be feared that the people will be exhausted, than that Government will not be supplied. Whereas, whatever is got by acts of absolute power, ill obeyed, because odious, or by contracts ill kept, because constrained, will be narrow, feeble, uncertain, and precarious. " Ease would retract vows made in pain, as violent and void."

I, for one, protest against compounding our demands : I declare against compounding, for a poor limited sum, the immense, ever-growing, eternal debt, which is due to generous government from protected freedom. And so may I speed in the great object I propose to you, as I think it would not only be an act of injustice, but would be the worst economy in the world, to compel the colonies to a sum certain, either in the way of ransom, or in the way of compulsory compact.

But to clear up my ideas on this subject—a revenue from America transmitted hither—do not delude yourselves : you never can receive it—no, not a shilling. We have experience that from re- mote countries it is not to be expected. If, when . you attempted to extract revenue from Bengal, you were obliged to return in loan what you had taken in imposition, what can you expect from North America ? For certainly, if ever there was a coun- try qualified to produce wealth, it is India ; or an institution for the transmission, it is the East India Company. America has none of these aptitudes. If America gives you taxable objects, on which you lay your duties here, and gives you, at the same time, a surplus by a foreign sale of her commodities to pay the duties on these objects, which you tax at home, she has performed her part to the British revenue. But with regard to her own internal establishments, she may—I doubt not she will—con- tribute in moderation. I say in moderation ; for she ought not to be permitted to exhaust herself. She ought to be reserved to a war ; the weight of which, with the enemies that we are most likely to have, must be considerable in her quarter of the globe. There she may serve you, and serve you essentially.

For that service, for all service, whether of revenue, trade, or empire, my trust is in her interest in the British Constitution. My hold of the colonies is in the close affection which grows from common names, from kindred blood, from similar privileges, and equal protection. These are ties which, though

light as air, are as strong as links of iron. Let the
colonies always keep the idea of their civil rights
associated with your government; they will cling
and grapple to you, and no force under heaven will
be of power to tear them from their allegiance. But
let it be once understood that your government may
be one thing and their privileges another; that these
two things may exist without any mutual relation;
the cement is gone, the cohesion is loosened, and
everything hastens to decay and dissolution. As
long as you have the wisdom to keep the sovereign
authority of this country as the sanctuary of liberty,
the sacred temple consecrated to our common faith,
wherever the chosen race and sons of England
worship freedom, they will turn their faces towards
you. The more they multiply, the more friends you
will have; the more ardently they love liberty, the
more perfect will be their obedience. Slavery they
can have anywhere. It is a weed that grows in
every soil. They may have it from Spain, they may
have it from Prussia. But, until you become lost to
all feeling of your true interest and your natural
dignity, freedom they can have from none but you.
This is the commodity of price, of which you have
the monopoly. This is the true Act of Navigation
which binds to you the commerce of the colonies,
and through them secures to you the wealth of the
world. Deny them this participation of freedom,
and you break that sole bond which originally made

and must still preserve the unity of the empire.
Do not entertain so weak an imagination as that
your registers and your bonds, your affidavits and
your sufferances, your cockets and your clearances,
are what form the great securities of your commerce.
Do not dream that your letters of office, and your
instructions, and your suspending clauses are the
things that hold together the great contexture of the
mysterious whole.   These things do not make your
government.   Dead instruments, passive tools as
they are, it is the spirit of the English communion
that gives all their life and efficacy to them.   It is
the spirit of the English Constitution, which, infused
through the mighty mass, pervades, feeds, unites,
invigorates, vivifies every part of the empire, even
down to the minutest member.

It is not the same virtue which does everything
for us here in England ?   Do you imagine, then, that
it is the Land Tax Act which raises your revenue ?
that it is the annual vote in the Committee of Supply
which gives you your army ? or that it is the Mutiny
Bill which inspires it with bravery and discipline ?
No ! surely no !   It is the love of the people : it is
their attachment to their Government, from the sense
of the deep stake they have in such a glorious
institution, which gives you your army and your
navy, and infuses into both that liberal obedience
without which your army would be a base rabble,
and your navy nothing but rotten timber.

All this, I know well enough, will sound wild and chimerical to the profane herd of those vulgar and mechanical politicians who have no place among us ; a sort of people who think that nothing exists but what is gross and material ; and who, therefore, far from being qualified to be directors of the great movement of empire, are not fit to turn a wheel in the machine. But to men truly initiated and rightly taught, these ruling and master principles, which in the opinion of such men as I have mentioned have no substantial existence, are in truth everything and all in all. Magnanimity in politics is not seldom the truest wisdom ; and a great empire and little minds go ill together. If we are conscious of our station, and glow with zeal to fill our places as becomes our situation and ourselves, we ought to auspicate all our public proceedings on America with the old warning of the church, *Sursum corda !* We ought to elevate our minds to the greatness of that trust to which the order of Providence has called us. By adverting to the dignity of this high calling, our ancestors have turned a savage wilderness into a glorious empire ; and have made the most extensive, and the only honourable conquests, not by destroying, but by promoting the wealth, the number, the happiness of the human race. Let us get an American revenue as we have got an American empire. English privileges have made it all that it is ; English privileges alone will make it all it can be.

In full confidence of this unalterable truth, I now (*quod felix faustumque sit*) lay the first stone of the Temple of Peace ; and I move you—

> " That the colonies and plantations of Great Britain in North America, consisting of fourteen separate governments, and containing two millions and upwards of free inhabitants, have not had the liberty and privilege of electing and sending any knights and burgesses or others to represent them in the high court of Parliament."

BURKE'S TWO LETTERS

ON

IRISH QUESTIONS.

— ·•·— -

TO SAMUEL SPAN, ESQ.

SIR,—I am honoured with your letter of the 13th, in answer to mine, which accompanied the resolutions of the House relative to the trade of Ireland.

You will be so good as to present my best respects to the Society, and to assure them that it was altogether unnecessary to remind me of the interest of the constituents. I have never regarded anything else since I had a seat in Parliament. Having frequently and maturely considered that interest, and stated it to myself in almost every point of view, I am persuaded that, under the present circumstances, I cannot more effectually pursue it than by giving all the support in my power to the propositions which I lately transmitted to the Hall.

The fault I find in the scheme is, that it falls extremely short of that liberality in the commercial

system which I trust will one day be adopted. If
I had not considered the present resolutions merely
as preparatory to better things, and as a means of
showing experimentally that justice to others is
not always folly to ourselves, I should have con-
tented myself with receiving them in a cold and
silent acquiescence. Separately considered, they
are matters of no very great importance. But
they aim, however imperfectly, at a right principle.
I submit to the restraint to appease prejudice ; I
accept the enlargement, so far as it goes, as the
result of reason and of sound policy.

We cannot be insensible of the calamities which
have been brought upon this nation by an obstinate
adherence to narrow and restrictive plans of government. I confess I cannot prevail on myself to take
them up precisely at a time when the most decisive
experience has taught the rest of the world to lay
them down. The propositions in question did not
originate from me, or from my particular friends.
But when things are so right in themselves, I hold
it my duty not to inquire from what hands they
come. I opposed the American measures upon
the very same principle on which I support those
that relate to Ireland. I was convinced that the
evils which have arisen from the adoption of the
former would be infinitely aggravated by the rejection of the latter.

Perhaps gentlemen are not yet fully aware of the

situation of their country, and what its exigencies absolutely require. I find that we are still disposed to talk at our ease, and as if all things were to be regulated by our good pleasure. I should consider it as a fatal symptom if, in our present distressed and adverse circumstances, we should persist in the errors which are natural only to prosperity. One cannot, indeed, sufficiently lament the continuance of that spirit of delusion by which, for a long time past, we have thought fit to measure our necessities by our inclinations. Moderation, prudence, and equity are far more suitable to our condition than loftiness, and confidence, and rigour. We are threatened by enemies of no small magnitude, whom, if we think fit, we may despise, as we have despised others ; but they are enemies who can only cease to be truly formidable by our entertaining a due respect for their power. Our danger will not be lessened by our shutting our eyes to it, nor will our force abroad be increased by rendering ourselves feeble and divided at home.

There is a dreadful schism in the British nation. Since we are not able to reunite the empire, it is our business to give all possible vigour and soundness to those parts of it which are still content to be governed by our councils. Sir, it is proper to inform you that our measures must be healing. Such a degree of strength must be communicated to all the members of the State as may enable them to

defend themselves, and to co-operate in the defence
of the whole. Their temper, too, must be managed
and their good affections cultivated. They may
then be disposed to bear the load with cheerfulness,
as a contribution towards what may be called with
truth and propriety, and not by an empty form of
words, a common cause. Too little dependence
cannot be had, at this time of day, on names and
prejudices. The eyes of mankind are opened ; and
communities must be held together by an evident
and solid interest. God forbid that our conduct
should demonstrate to the world that Great Britain
can, in no instance whatsoever, be brought to a
sense of rational and equitable policy but by
coercion and force of arms !

I wish you to recollect, with what powers of concession, relatively to commerce as well as to legislation, his Majesty's Commissioners to the united
colonies have sailed from England within this week·
Whether these powers are sufficient for their purposes it is not now my business to examine ; but
we all know that our resolutions in favour of Ireland
are trifling and insignificant when compared with the
concessions to the Americans. At such a juncture
I would implore every man, who retains the least
spark of regard to the yet remaining honour and
security of this country, not to compel others to
an imitation of their conduct, or by passion and
violence to force them to seek in the territories of

the separation that freedom and those advantages which they are not to look for whilst they remain under the wings of their ancient government.

After all, what are the matters we dispute with so much warmth? Do we in these resolutions bestow anything upon Ireland? Not a shilling. We only consent to leave to them, in two or three instances, the use of the natural faculties which God has given to them and to all mankind. Is Ireland united to the Crown of Great Britain for no other purpose than that we should counteract the bounty of Providence in her favour? And in proportion as that bounty has been liberal that we are to regard it as an evil, which is to be met with in every sort of corrective? To say that Ireland interferes with us and therefore must be checked, is, in my opinion, a very mistaken and a very dangerous principle. I must beg leave to repeat, what I took the liberty of suggesting to you in my last letter, that Ireland is a country in the same climate, and of the same natural qualities and productions with this, and has consequently no other means of growing wealthy in herself, or, in other words, of being useful to us, but by doing the very same things which we do for the same purposes. I hope that in Great Britain we shall always pursue, without exception, every means of prosperity, and, of course, that Ireland will interfere with us in something or other; for either, in order to limit

her, we must restrain ourselves, or we must fall
into that shocking conclusion that we are to keep
our yet remaining dependency under a general and
indiscriminate restraint for the mere purpose of
oppression.   Indeed, Sir, England and Ireland may
flourish together.   The world is large enough for
us both.   Let it be our care not to make ourselves
too little for it.

I know it is said that the people of Ireland do
not pay the same taxes, and therefore ought not
in equity to enjoy the same benefits with this.   I
had hopes that the unhappy phantom of a compulsory equal taxation had haunted us long enough.
I do assure you that until it is entirely banished
from our imaginations (where alone it has or can
have any existence) we shall never cease to do
ourselves the most substantial injuries.   To that
argument of equal taxation I can only say that
Ireland pays as many taxes as those who are the
best judges of her powers are of opinion she can
bear.   To bear more she must have more ability;
and in the order of Nature, the advantage must
precede the charge.   This disposition of things,
being the law of God, neither you nor I can alter
it.   So that if you will have more help from Ireland
you must previously supply her with more means.
I believe it will be found that if men are suffered
freely to cultivate their natural advantages, a virtual
equality of contribution will come in its own time,

and will flow by an easy descent through its own
proper and natural channels. An attempt to disturb
that course and to force Nature will only bring on
universal discontent, distress and confusion.

You tell me, Sir, that you prefer a union with
Ireland to the little regulations which are proposed
in Parliament. This union is a great question of
State, to which, when it comes properly before me
in my parliamentary capacity, I shall give an honest
and unprejudiced consideration. However, it is a
settled rule with me to make the most of my actual
situation, and not to refuse to do a proper thing
because there is something else more proper which
I am not able to do. This union is a business of
difficulty, and on the principles of your letter a
business impracticable. Until it can be matured
into a feasible and desirable scheme, I wish to
have as close a union of interest and affection with
Ireland as I can have ; and that, I am sure, is a
far better thing than any nominal union of government.

France, and indeed most extensive empires, which
by various designs and fortunes have grown into one
great mass, contain many provinces that are very
different from each other in privileges and modes
of government; and they raise their supplies in
different ways, in different proportions, and under
different authorities, yet none of them are for this
reason curtailed of their natural rights, but they

carry on trade and manufactures with perfect
equality. In some way or other the true balance
is found, and all of them are properly poised and
harmonized. How much have you lost by the
participation of Scotland in all your commerce?
The external trade of England has more than
doubled since that period, and I believe your
internal (which is the most advantageous) has
been augmented at least fourfold. Such virtue
there is in liberality of sentiment that you have
grown richer even by the partnership of poverty.

If you think that this participation was a loss,
commercially considered, but that it has been com-
pensated by the share which Scotland has taken in
defraying the public charge, I believe you have not
very carefully looked at the public accounts. Ireland,
Sir, pays a great deal more than Scotland, and is
perhaps as much and as effectually united to
England as Scotland is. But if Scotland, instead
of paying little, had paid nothing at all, we should
be gainers, not losers, by acquiring the hearty co-
operation of an active, intelligent people towards
the increase of the common stock, instead of our
being employed in watching and counteracting
them, and their being employed in watching and
counteracting us, with the peevish and churlish
jealousy of rivals and enemies on both sides.

I am sure, Sir, that the commercial experience
of the merchants of Bristol will soon disabuse them

of the prejudice that they can trade no longer, if countries more lightly taxed are permitted to deal in the same commodities at the same markets. You know that, in fact, you trade very largely where you are met by the goods of all nations. You even pay high duties on the import of your goods, and afterwards undersell nations less taxed at their own markets, and where goods of the same kind are not charged at all. If it were otherwise, you could trade very little. You know that the price of all sorts of manufacture is not a great deal enhanced (except to the domestic consumer) by any taxes paid in this country. This I might very easily prove.

The same consideration will relieve you from the apprehension you express with relation to sugars, and the difference of the duties paid here and in Ireland. Those duties affect the interior consumer only; and for obvious reasons, relative to the interest of revenue itself, they must be proportioned to his ability of payment; but in all cases in which sugar can be an object of commerce, and therefore (in this view) of rivalship, you are sensible that you are at least on a par with Ireland. As to your apprehensions concerning the more advantageous situation of Ireland for some branches of commerce (for it is so but for some), I trust you will not find them more serious. Milford Haven, which is at your door, may serve to show you that the mere advantage of ports is not the thing which shifts the seat of commerce from one part of the world to the other. If I thought you inclined to take up this matter on local considerations, I should state to you that I do not know any part of the kingdom so well situated for an advantageous commerce with Ireland as Bristol ; and that none would be so likely to profit of its prosperity as our city. But your profit and theirs must concur. Beggary and bankruptcy are not the circumstances which invite to an intercourse with that or with any country ; and I believe it will be found invariably true that the superfluities of a rich nation furnish a better object of trade than the necessities of a poor one. It is the interest of the commercial world that wealth should be found everywhere.

The true ground of fear, in my opinion, is this : that Ireland, from the vicious system of its internal polity, will be a long time before it can derive any benefit from the liberty now granted or from anything else. But as I do not vote advantages, in hopes that they may not be enjoyed, I will not lay any stress upon this consideration. I rather wish that the Parliament of Ireland may, in its own wisdom, remove these impediments, and put their country in a condition to avail itself of its natural advantages. If they do not, the fault is with them and not with us.

I have written this long letter in order to give

all possible satisfaction to my constituents with
regard to the part I have taken in this affair. It
gave me inexpressible concern to find that my
conduct has been a cause of uneasiness to any of
them. Next to my honour and conscience, I have
nothing so near and dear to me as their approbation.
However, I had much rather run the risk of displeasing than of injuring them, if I am driven to
make such an option. You obligingly lament that
you are not to have me for your advocate ; but if
I had been capable of acting as an advocate in
opposition to a plan so perfectly consonant to my
known principles, and to the opinions I had publicly
declared on a hundred occasions, I should only disgrace myself without supporting, with the smallest
degree of credit or effect, the cause you wished me
to undertake. I should have lost the only thing
which can make such abilities as mine of any use
to the world now or hereafter—I mean that authority
which is derived from an opinion that a member
speaks the language of truth and sincerity, and
that he is not ready to take up or lay down a great
political system for the convenience of the hour ;
that he is in Parliament to support his opinion of
the public good, and does not form his opinion in
order to get into Parliament or to continue in it.
It is in a great measure for your sake that I wish
to preserve this character. Without it, I am sure
I should be ill able to discharge, by any service,

the smallest part of that debt of gratitude and affection which I owe you for the great and honourable trust you have reposed in me.

I am, with the highest regard and esteem,

Sir, your most obedient

And humble servant,

E. B.

Beaconsfield,

April 23, 1778

TO SIR HERCULES LANGRISHE, M.P.

MY DEAR SIR,—Your rémembrance of me, with sentiments of so much kindness, has given me the most sincere satisfaction. It perfectly agrees with the friendly and hospitable reception which my son and I received from you, some time since, when after an absence of twenty-two years, I had the happiness of embracing you, among my few surviving friends.

I really imagined that I should not again interest myself in any public business. I had, to the best of my moderate faculties, paid my club to the society, which I was born in some way or other to serve ; and I thought I had a right to put on my night-gown and slippers, and with a cheerful evening to the good company I must leave behind. But if our resolutions of vigour and exertion are so often broken or pro-crastinated in the execution, I think we may be excused, if we are not very punctual in fulfilling our engagements to indolence and inactivity. I have indeed no power of action, and am almost a cripple even with regard to thinking ; but you descend with force into the stagnant pool, and you cause such a fermentation as to cure at least one impotent creature

of his lameness, though it cannot enable him either
to run or to wrestle.

You see by the paper I take that I am likely to be
long, with *malice prepense*. You have brought under
my view a subject, always difficult, at present critical.
It has filled my thoughts, which I wish to lay open
to you with the clearness and simplicity which your
friendship demands from me. I thank you for the
communication of your ideas. I should be still more
pleased if they had been more your own. What
you hint, I believe to be the case ; that if you had
not deferred to the judgment of others, our opinions
would not differ more materially at this day than
they did when we used to confer on the same subject
so many years ago. If I still persevere in my old
opinions, it is no small comfort to me, that it is
not with regard to doctrines properly yours that I
discover my indocility.

The case upon which your letter of the 10th of
December turns is hardly before me with precision
enough to enable me to form any very certain
judgment upon it. It seems to be some plan of
further indulgence proposed for Catholics of Ireland.
You observe that your "general principles are not
changed, but that times and circumstances are
altered." I perfectly agree with you, that times and
circumstances, considered with reference to the public,
ought very much to govern our conduct ; though I
am far from slighting, when applied with discretion

to those circumstances, general principles and maxims of policy. I cannot help observing, however, that you have said rather less upon the inapplicability of your. own old principles to the circumstances that are likely to influence your conduct against these principles, than of the general maxims of State, which I can very readily believe not to have great weight with you personally.

In my present state of imperfect information, you will pardon the errors into which I may easily fall. The principles you lay down are, "that the Roman Catholics should enjoy everything under the State, but should not be the State itself." And you add, "that when you exclude them from being a part of the State, you rather conform to the spirit of the age, than to any abstract doctrine ;" but you consider the Constitution as already established—that our State is Protestant. "It was declared so at the Revolution. It was so provided in the Acts for settling the succession of the Crown : the king's coronation oath was enjoined in order to keep it so. The king, as first magistrate of the State, is obliged to take the oath of abjuration, and to subscribe the declaration ; and, by laws subsequent, every other magistrate and member of the State, legislative and executive, are bound under the same obligation."

As to the plan to which these maxims are applied, I cannot speak, as I told you, positively about it ; because, neither from your letter, nor from any information I have been able to collect, do I find anything settled, either on the part of the Roman Catholics themselves, or on that of any persons who may wish to conduct their affairs in Parliament. But if I have leave to conjecture, something is in agitation towards admitting them, under certain qualifications, to have some share in the election of members of Parliament. This I understand is the scheme of those who are entitled to come within your description of persons of consideration, property, and character ; and firmly attached to the King and Constitution as by "law established, with a grateful sense of your former concessions, and a patient reliance on the benignity of Parliament, for the further mitigation of the laws that still affect them." As to the low, thoughtless, wild, and profligate, who have joined themselves with those of other professions, but of the same character, you are not to imagine that for a moment I can suppose them to be met with anything else than the manly and enlightened energy of a firm Government, supported by the united efforts of all virtuous men, if ever their proceedings should become so considerable as to demand its notice. I really think that such associations should be crushed in their very commencement.

Setting, therefore, this case out of the question, it becomes an object of very serious consideration, whether, because wicked men of various descriptions

are engaged in seditious courses, the rational, sober,
and valuable part of one description should not be
indulged in their sober and rational expectations?
You, who have looked deeply into the spirit of the
Popery laws, must be perfectly sensible that a great
part of the present mischief, which we abhor in
common (if it at all exists), has arisen from them.
Their declared object was to reduce the Catholics of
Ireland to a miserable populace, without property,
without estimation, without education. The professed object was to deprive the few men who, in
spite of those laws, might hold or obtain any property amongst them, of all sort of influence or
authority over the rest. They divided the nation
into two distinct bodies, without common interest,
sympathy, or connection. One of these bodies was
to possess all the franchises, all the property, all the
education ; the other was to be composed of drawers
of water and cutters of turf for them. Are we to
be astonished, when, by the efforts of so much violence
in conquest, and so much policy in regulation, continued without intermission for near a hundred
years, we had reduced them to a mob ; that whenever
they came to act at all, many of them would act
exactly like a mob, without temper, measure, or
foresight ? Surely it might be just now a matter of
temperate discussion, whether you ought not to apply a
remedy to the real cause of the evil. If the disorder
you speak of be real and considerable, you ought to

raise an aristocratic interest—that is, an interest of
property and education amongst them ; and to
strengthen by every prudent means the authority
and influence of men of that description.   It will
deserve your best thoughts, to examine whether this
can be done without giving such persons the means
of demonstrating to the rest that something more is
to be got by their temperate conduct than can be
expected from the wild and senseless projects of
those who do not belong to their body, who have
no interest in their well-being, and only wish to
make them the dupes of their turbulent ambition.

If the absurd persons you mention find no way of
providing for liberty but by overturning this happy
Constitution, and introducing a frantic democracy, let
us take care how we prevent better people from any
rational expectations of partaking in the benefits of
that Constitution as it stands.   The maxims you
establish cut the matter short.   They have no sort
of connection with the good or the ill behaviour of
the persons who seek relief, or with the proper or
improper means by which they seek it.   They form
a perpetual bar to all pleas and to all expectations.

You begin by asserting that "the Catholics ought
to enjoy all things under the State, but that they
ought not to be the State ;" a position which, I
believe, in the latter part of it, and in the latitude
there expressed, no man of common sense has ever
thought proper to dispute, because the contrary

implies that the State ought to be in them exclu-
sively. But before you have finished the line, you
express yourself as if the other member of your
proposition—namely, that "they ought not to be a
part of the State"—were necessarily included in your
first; whereas I conceive it to be as different as a
part is from the whole—that is, just as different as
possible. I know, indeed, that it is common with
those who talk very differently from you—that is, with
heat and animosity—to confound those things, and to
argue the admission of the Catholics into any, however minute and subordinate parts of the State, as a
surrender into their hands of the whole government
of the kingdom. To them I have nothing at all to
say.

Wishing to proceed with a deliberative spirit and
temper in so very serious a question, I shall attempt
to analyze, as well as I can, the principles you lay
down, in order to fit them for the grasp of an understanding so little comprehensive as mine—"State,"
"Protestant," "Revolution." These are terms which,
if not well explained, may lead us into many errors.
In the word State I conceive there is much am-
biguity. The State is sometimes used to signify
the whole commonwealth, comprehending all its
orders, with the several privileges belonging to each.
Sometimes it signifies only the higher and ruling
part of the commonwealth, which we commonly
call the Government. In the first sense, to be under

the State, but not the State itself, nor any part of it—
that is, to be nothing at all in the commonwealth—is
a situation perfectly intelligible ; but to those who
feel that situation not very pleasant, when it is
understood.   It is a state of civil servitude by the
very force of the definition.   *Servorum non est
respublica* is a very old and a very true maxim.
This servitude, which makes men subject to a State
without being citizens, may be more or less tolerable
from many circumstances ; but these circumstances,
more or less favourable, do not alter the nature of
the thing.   The mildness by which absolute masters
exercise their dominion, leaves them masters still.
We may talk a little presently of the manner in
which the majority of the people of Ireland (the
Catholics) are affected by this situation, which at
present undoubtedly is theirs, and which you are of
opinion ought so to continue for ever.

In the other sense of the word State, by which is
understood the Supreme Government only, I must
observe this upon the question, that to exclude
whole classes of men entirely from this part of
government cannot be considered as absolute
slavery.   It only implies a lower and degraded
state of citizenship ; such is—with more or less
strictness—-the condition of all countries in which
an hereditary nobility possess the exclusive rule.
This may be no bad mode of government, provided
that the personal authority of individual nobles be

kept in due bounds, that their cabals and factions are guarded against with a severe vigilance, and that the people—who have no share in granting their own money—are subjected to but light impositions, and are otherwise treated with attention, and with indulgence to their humours and prejudices.

The republic of Venice is one of those which strictly confines all the great functions and offices, such as are truly State functions and State offices, to those who, by hereditary right or admission, are noble Venetians. But there are many offices, and some of them not mean nor unprofitable, which are reserved for the Citadini. Of these all citizens of Venice are capable. The inhabitants of the *terra firma*, who are mere subjects of conquest—that is, as you express it, under the State, but "not a part of it"—are not, however, subjects in so very rigorous a sense as not to be capable of numberless subordinate employments. It is indeed one of the advantages attending the narrow bottom of their aristocracy (narrow as compared with their acquired dominions, otherwise broad enough) that an exclusion from such employments cannot possibly be made amongst their subjects. There are, besides, advantages in States so constituted, by which those who are considered as of an inferior race are indemnified for their exclusion from the government and from noble employments. In all these countries, either by express law or by usage more operative, the noble castes are almost

universally, in their turn, excluded from commerce,
manufacture, farming of land, and in general from
all lucrative civil professions. The nobles have the
monopoly of honour. The plebeians a monopoly of
all the means of acquiring wealth. Thus some sort
of a balance is formed among conditions ; a sort of
compensation is furnished to those who, in a limited
sense, are excluded from the government of the
State.

Between the extreme of a total exclusion, to which
your maxim goes, and a universal unmodified capacity
to which the fanatics pretend, there are many different degrees and stages, and a great variety of
temperaments, upon which prudence may give full
scope to its exertions. For you know that the
decisions of prudence (contrary to the system of the
insane reasoners) differ from those of judicature ; and
that almost all the former are determined on the
more or the less, the earlier or the later, and on a
balance of advantage and inconvenience, of good and
evil.

In all considerations which turn upon the question
of vesting or continuing the State solely and exclu-
sively in some one description of citizens, prudent
legislators will consider how far the general form
and principles of their commonwealth render it fit to
be cast into an oligarchical shape, or to remain
always in it. We know that the Government of
Ireland (the same as the British) is not in its

constitution wholly aristocratical ; and as it is not
such in its form, so neither is it in its spirit. If it
had been inveterately aristocratical, exclusions might
be more patiently submitted to. The lot of one
plebeian would be the lot of all ; and an habitual
reverence and admiration of certain families might
make the people content to see government wholly
in hands to whom it seemed naturally to belong.
But our Constitution has a plebeian member, which
forms an essential integrant part of it. A plebeian
oligarchy is a monster ; and no people, not absolutely
domestic or predial slaves, will long endure it. The
Protestants of Ireland are not alone sufficiently the
people to form a democracy ; and they are too
numerous to answer the ends and purposes of an
aristocracy. Admiration, that first source of obedience, can be only the claim or the imposture of the
few. I hold it to be absolutely impossible for two
millions of plebeians, composing certainly a very
clear and decided majority in that class, to become
so far in love with six or seven hundred thousand of
their fellow-citizens (to all outward appearance
plebeians like themselves, and many of them trades-
men, servants, and otherwise inferior to some of
them) as to see with satisfaction, or even with
patience, an exclusive power vested in them, by
which constitutionally they become the absolute
masters ; and by the manners derived from their
circumstances, must be capable of exercising upon

them, daily and hourly, an insulting and vexatious
superiority.   Neither are the majority of the Irish
indemnified (as in some aristocracies) for this state
of humiliating vassalage (often inverting the nature
of things and relations) by having the lower walks
of industry wholly abandoned to them.   They are
rivalled, to say the least of the matter, in every
laborious and lucrative course of life ; while every
franchise, every honour, every trust, every place,
down to the very lowest and least confidential
(besides whole professions), is reserved for the
master-caste.

Our Constitution is not made for great, general,
and proscriptive exclusions ; sooner or later it will
destroy them, or they will destroy the Constitution.
In our Constitution there has always been a difference
made between a franchise and an office, and between
the capacity for the one and for the other.   Franchises were supposed to belong to the subject as a
subject, and not as a member of the governing part
of the State.   The policy of government has considered them as things very different ; for whilst
Parliament excluded by the Test Acts (and for a
while these Test Acts were not a dead letter, as now
they are in England) Protestant dissenters from all
civil and military employments, they never touched
their right of voting for members of Parliament, or
sitting in either House ; a point I state, not as
approving or condemning, with regard to them, the

measure of exclusion from employments, but to prove that the distinction has been admitted in legislature, as, in truth, it is founded in reason.

I will not here examine whether the principles of the British [the Irish] Constitution be wise or not. I must assume that they are ; and that those who partake the franchises which make it, partake of a benefit. They who are excluded from votes (under proper qualifications inherent in the Constitution that gives them) are excluded, not from the State, but from the British Constitution. They cannot by any possibility, whilst they hear its praises continually rung in their ears, and are present at the declaration which is so generally and so bravely made by those who possess the privilege—that the best blood in their veins ought to be shed, to preserve their share in it ; they, the disfranchised part, cannot, I say, think themselves in a happy state, to be utterly excluded from all its direct and all its consequential advantages. The popular part of the Constitution must be to them by far the most odious part of it. To them it is not an actual, and, if possible, still less a virtual representation. It is indeed the direct contrary. It is power unlimited, placed in the hands of an adverse description, because it is an adverse description. And if they who compose the privileged body have not an interest, they must but too frequently have motives of pride, passion, petulance, peevish jealousy, or tyrannic suspicion, to urge them to treat the excluded people with contempt and rigour.

This is not a mere theory ; though whilst men are men, it is a theory that cannot be false. I do not desire to revive all the particulars in my memory ; I wish them to sleep for ever ; but it is impossible I should wholly forget what happened in some parts of Ireland, with very few and short intermissions, from the year 1761 to the year 1766, both inclusive. In a country of miserable police, passing from the extremes of laxity to the extremes of rigour, among a neglected and therefore disorderly populace—if any disturbance or sedition, from any grievance real or imaginary, happened to arise, it was presently perverted from its true nature, often criminal enough in itself to draw upon it a severe appropriate punishment ; it was metamorphosed into a conspiracy against the State, and prosecuted as such. Amongst the Catholics, as being by far the most numerous and the most wretched, all sorts of offenders against the laws must commonly be found. The punishment of low people for the offences usual amongst low people, would warrant no inference against any descriptions of religion or of politics. Men of consideration from their age, their profession, or their character ; men of proprietary landed estates, substantial renters, opulent merchants, physicians, and titular bishops, could not easily be suspected of riot in open day, or of nocturnal assemblies for the

purpose of pulling down hedges, making breaches in
park walls, firing barns, maiming cattle, and outrages
of a similar nature, which characterize the disorders
of an oppressed or a licentious populace.   But when
the evidence given on the trial for such mis-
demeanours, qualified them as overt acts of high
treason, and when witnesses were found (such
witnesses as they were) to depose to the taking of
oaths of allegiance by the rioters to the King of
France, to their being paid by his money, and
embodied and exercised under his officers, to overturn the State for the purposes of that potentate ;
in that case, the rioters might (if the witness was
believed) be supposed only the troops, and persons
more reputable, the leaders and commanders in such
a rebellion.   All classes in the obnoxious description
who could not be suspected of the lower crime of
riot, might be involved in the odium, in the suspicion, and sometimes in the punishment, of a
higher and far more criminal species of offence.
These proceedings did not arise from any one of
the Popery laws since repealed, but from this circumstance, that when it answered the purposes
of an election party, or a malevolent person of
influence to forge such plots, the people had no
protection.   The people of that description have
no hold on the gentlemen who aspire to be popular
representatives.   The candidates neither love, nor
respect, nor fear them, individually or collec-

tively. I do not think this evil (an evil amongst a thousand others) at this day entirely over; for I conceive I have lately seen some indication of a disposition perfectly similar to the old one; that is, a disposition to carry the imputation of crimes from persons to descriptions, and wholly to alter the character and quality of the offences themselves.

This universal exclusion seems to me a serious evil—because many collateral oppressions, besides what I have just now stated, have arisen from it. In things of this nature, it would not be either easy or proper to quote chapter and verse; but I have great reason to believe, particularly since the Octennial Act, that several have refused at all to let their lands to Roman Catholics; because it would so far disable them from promoting such interests in counties as they were inclined to favour. They who consider also the state of all sorts of trades-men, shopkeepers, and particularly publicans in towns, must soon discern the disadvantages under which those labour who have no votes. It cannot be otherwise whilst the spirit of elections and the tendencies of human nature continue as they are. If property be artificially separated from franchise, the franchise must in some way or other, and in some proportion, naturally attract property to it. Many are the collateral disadvantages, amongst a privileged people, which must attend on those who have no privileges.

Among the rich, each individual, with or without
a franchise, is of importance ; the poor and the
middling are no otherwise so than as they obtain
some collective capacity, and can be aggregated to
some corps.   If legal ways are not found, illegal
will be resorted to ;   and seditious clubs and con-
federacies, such as no man living holds in greater
horror than I do, will grow and flourish, in spite, I
am afraid, of anything which can be done to prevent
the evil.   Lawful enjoyment is the surest method
to prevent unlawful gratification.   Where there is
property, there will be less theft ; where there is
marriage, there will always be less fornication.

I have said enough of the question of State, as it
affects the people, merely as such.   But it is complicated with a political question relative to religion,
to which it is very necessary I should say something ;
because the term Protestant, which you apply, is too
general for the conclusions which one of your accurate
understanding would wish to draw from it ; and because a great deal of argument will depend on the
use that is made of that term.

It is not a fundamental part of the settlement at
the Revolution that the State should be Protestant
without any qualification of the term.   With a
qualification it is unquestionably true; not in all
its latitude.   With the qualification, it was true before the Revolution.   Our predecessors in legislation
were not so irrational (not to say impious) as to

form an operose ecclesiastical establishment, and even
to render the State itself in some degree subservient
to it, when their religion (if such it might be called)
was nothing but a mere negation of some other—
without any positive idea either of doctrine, discipline,
worship, or morals, in the scheme which they professed themselves, and which they imposed upon
others, even under penalties and incapacities.   No,
no! This never could have been done even by
reasonable atheists.   They who think religion of no
importance to the State have abandoned it to the
conscience or caprice of the individual ; they make
no provision for it whatsoever, but leave every club
to make, or not, a voluntary contribution towards its
support, according to their fancies.   This would be
consistent.   The other always appeared to me to be
a monster of contradiction and absurdity.   It was
for that reason that some years ago I strenuously
opposed the clergy who petitioned, to the number of
about three hundred, to be freed from the subscrip-
tion to the Thirty-nine Articles, without proposing to
substitute any other in their place.   There never has
been a religion of the State (the few years of the
Parliament only excepted) but that of the Episcopal
Church of England—the Episcopal Church of England before the Reformation connected with the See
of Rome ; since then, disconnected, and protesting
against some of her doctrines, and against the whole
of her authority, as binding in our National Church :

nor did the fundamental laws of this kingdom (in
Ireland it has been the same) ever know, at any
period, any other Church as an object of Establishment, or in that light any other Protestant religion.
Nay, our Protestant toleration itself at the Revolution,
and until within a few years, required a signature of
thirty-six, and a part of a thirty-seventh, out of the
Thirty-nine Articles. So little idea had they at the
Revolution of establishing Protestantism indefinitely,
that they did not indefinitely tolerate it under that
name. I do not mean to praise that strictness,
where nothing more than merely religious toleration
is concerned. Toleration being a part of moral and
political prudence, ought to be tender and large. A
tolerant Government ought not to be too scrupulous
in its investigations ; but may bear without blame,
not only very ill-grounded doctrines, but even many
things that are positively vices, where they are
adulta et prævalida. The good of the commonwealth is the rule which rides over the rest, and to
this every other must completely submit.

The Church of Scotland knows as little of Protestantism, undefined, as the Churches of England and
Ireland do. She has by the Articles of Union secured
to herself the perpetual establishment of the Confession of Faith, and the Presbyterian Church government. In England, even during the troubled inter-
regnum, it was not thought fit to establish a negative
religion, but the Parliament settled the Presbyterian

as the Church discipline, the Directory as the rule of
public worship, and the Westminster Catechism as
the institute of faith. This is to show that at no
time was the Protestant religion, undefined, established here, or anywhere else, as I believe. I am
sure that when the three religions were established
in Germany, they were expressly characterized and
declared to be the Evangelic, the Reformed, and the
Catholic, each of which has its confession of faith
and its settled discipline ; so that you always may
know the best and the worst of them, to enable you
to make the most of what is good, and to correct, or
to qualify, or to guard against whatever may seem
evil or dangerous.

As to the coronation oath, to which you allude,
as opposite to admitting a Roman Catholic to the
use of any franchise whatsoever, I cannot think that
the king would be perjured if he gave his assent to
any regulation which Parliament might think fit to
make with regard to that affair. The king is
bound by law, as clearly specified in several Acts of
Parliament, to be in communion with the Church of
England. It is a part of the tenure by which he
holds his crown ; and though no provision was made
till the Revolution, which could be called positive
and valid in law, to ascertain this great principle, I
have always considered it as in fact fundamental,
that the King of England should be of the Christian
religion, according to the national legal church for

the time being. I conceive it was so before the
Reformation. Since the Reformation it became
doubly necessary, because the king is the head of
that church—in some sort an ecclesiastical person ;
and it would be incongruous and absurd to have the
head of the church of one faith, and the members of
another. The king may inherit the crown as a
Protestant, but he cannot hold it according to law,
without being a Protestant of the Church of
England.

Before we take it for granted that the king is
bound by his coronation oath not to admit any of
his Catholic subjects to the rights and liberties
which ought to belong to them as Englishmen (not
as religionists), or to settle the conditions or proportions of such admission by an Act of Parliament, I
wish you to place before your eyes that oath itself,
as it is settled in the Act of William and Mary :

> "Will you to the utmost of your power main-
> tain the laws of God, the true profession of the
> Gospel, and the Protestant reformed religion as
> it is established by law? And will you preserve
> unto bishops and clergy, and the churches com-
> mitted to their charge, all such rights and
> privileges as by law do or shall appertain to
> them, or any of them?—All this I promise to do."

Here are the coronation engagements of the king.
In them I do not find one word to preclude his
Majesty from consenting to any arrangement which

Parliament may make with regard to the civil privileges of any part of his subjects.

It may not be amiss, on account of the light which it will throw on this discussion, to look a little more narrowly into the matter of that oath, in order to discover how far it has hitherto operated, or how far in future it ought to operate, as a bar to any proceedings of the Crown and Parliament in favour of those against whom it may be supposed that the king has engaged to support the Protestant Church of England in the two kingdoms in which it is established by law. First, the king swears he will maintain to the utmost of his power "the laws of God." I suppose it means the natural moral laws. Secondly, he swears to maintain "the true profession of the Gospel." By which I suppose is understood affirmatively the Christian religion. Thirdly, that he will maintain "the Protestant reformed religion." This leaves me no power of supposition or conjecture ; for that Protestant reformed religion is defined and described by the subsequent words, " established by law," and in this instance, to define it beyond all possibility of doubt, he "swears to maintain the bishops and clergy, and the churches committed to their charge," in their rights present and future.

This oath as effectually prevents the king from doing anything to the prejudice of the Church in favour of sectaries, Jews, Mahometans, or plain avowed infidels, as if he should do the same thing

in favour of the Catholics. You will see that it is
the same Protestant Church, so described, which the
king is to maintain and communicate with, according to the Act of Settlement of the 12th and 13th
of William III. The Act of the 5th of Anne,
made in prospect of the union, is entitled " An Act
for securing the Church of England as by law established." It meant to guard the Church implicitly
against any other mode of Protestant religion which
might creep in by means of the union. It proves
beyond all doubt, that the Legislature did not mean
to guard the Church on one part only, and to leave
it defenceless and exposed upon every other. This
Church, in that Act, is declared to be " fundamental
and essential" for ever, in the Constitution of the
United Kingdom, so far as England is concerned ;
and I suppose, as the law stands, even since the
independence, it is so in Ireland.

All this shows that the religion which the king is
bound to maintain has a positive part in it as well
as a negative, and that the positive part of it (in
which we are in perfect agreement with the Catholics
and with the Church of Scotland) is infinitely the
most valuable and essential. Such an agreement
we had with Protestant Dissenters in England, of
those descriptions who came under the Toleration
Act of King William and Queen Mary—an Act
coeval with the Revolution, and which ought, on
the principles of the gentlemen who oppose the

relief to the Catholics, to have been held sacred and unalterable. Whether we agree with the present Protestant Dissenters in the points at the Revolution held essential and fundamental among Christians, or in any other fundamental, at present it is impossible for us to know ; because, at their own very earnest desire, we have repealed the Toleration Act of William and Mary, and discharged them from the signature required by that Act, and because, for the far greater part, they publicly declare against all manner of confessions of faith, even the consensus.

For reasons forcible enough at all times, but at this time particularly forcible with me, I dwell a little the longer upon this matter, and take the more pains to put us both in mind that it was not settled at the Revolution that the State should be Protestant in the latitude of the term, but in a defined and limited sense only, and that in that sense only the king is sworn to maintain it. To suppose that the king has sworn with his utmost power to maintain what it is wholly out of his power to discover, or which, if he could discover, he might discover to consist of things directly contradictory to each other, some of them perhaps impious, blasphemous, and seditious upon principle, would be not only a gross, but a most mischievous absurdity. If mere dissent from the Church of Rome be a merit, he that dissents the most perfectly is the most meritorious. In many points we hold strongly with that Church.

He that dissents throughout with that Church will dissent with the Church of England, and then it will be a part of his merit that he dissents with ourselves : a whimsical species of merit for any set of men to establish. We quarrel to extremity with those who we know agree with us in many things, but we are to be so malicious, even in the principle of our friendships, that we are to cherish in our bosom those who accord with us in nothing, because whilst they despise ourselves, they abhor even more than we do those with whom we have some disagreement. A man is certainly the most perfect Protestant who protests against the whole Christian religion. Whether a person's having no Christian religion be a title to favour, in exclusion to the largest description of Christians who hold all the doctrines of Christianity, though holding along with them some errors and some superfluities, is rather more than any man who has not become recreant and apostate from his baptism, will, I believe, choose to affirm. The countenance given from a spirit of controversy to that negative religion, may by degrees encourage light and unthinking people to a total indifference to everything positive in matters of doctrine, and, in the end, of practice too. If continued, it would play the game of that sort of active, proselytising, and persecuting atheism which is the disgrace and calamity of our time, and which we see to be as capable of subverting a Government as any mode can be of misguided zeal for better things.

Now let us fairly see what course has been taken relative to those against whom, in part at least, the king has sworn to maintain a church, positive in its doctrine and its discipline. The first thing done, even when the oath was fresh in the mouth of the sovereigns, was to give a toleration to Protestant Dissenters, whose doctrines they ascertained. As to the mere civil privileges which the Dissenters held as subjects before the Revolution, these were not touched at all. The laws have fully permitted, in a qualification for all offices, to such Dissenters an occasional conformity ; a thing I believe singular, where tests are admitted. The Act called the Test Act, itself is, with regard to them, grown to be hardly anything more than a dead letter. Whenever the Dissenters cease by their conduct to give any alarm to the Government in Church and State, I think it very probable that even this matter, rather disgustful than inconvenient to them, may be removed, or at least so modified as to distinguish the qualification to those offices which really guide the State from those which are merely instrumental, or that some other and better tests may be put in their place.

So far as to England. In Ireland you have outrun us. Without waiting for an English example, you have totally and without any modification whatsoever, repealed the test as to Protestant

Dissenters. Not having the repealing Act by me, I ought not to say positively that there is no exception in it; but if it be what I suppose it is, you know very well that a Jew in religion, or a Mahometan, or even a public, declared atheist and blasphemer, is perfectly qualified to be lord lieutenant, a lord justice, or even keeper of the king's conscience; and by virtue of his office (if with you it be as it is with us) administrator to a great part of the ecclesiastical patronage of the Crown.

Now let us deal a little fairly. We must admit that Protestant dissent was one of the quarters from which danger was apprehended at the Revolution, and against which a part of the coronation oath was peculiarly directed. By this unqualified repeal you certainly did not mean to deny that it was the duty of the Crown to preserve the Church against Protestant Dissenters; or, taking this to be the true sense of the two Revolution Acts of King William, and of the previous and subsequent Union Acts of Queen Anne, you did not declare by this most unqualified repeal, by which you broke down all the barriers, not invented, indeed, but carefully preserved at the Revolution; you did not then and by that proceeding declare that you had advised the king to perjury towards God and perfidy towards the Church. No! far, very far from it! You never would have done it, if you did not think it could be done with perfect repose to the royal conscience and perfect safety to

the national established religion. You did this upon
a full consideration of the circumstances of your
country. Now, if circumstances required it, why
should it be contrary to the king's oath, his Parliament judging on those circumstances, to restore to
his Catholic people in such measure and with such
modifications as the public wisdom shall think
proper to add, some part in these franchises which
they formerly had held without any limitation at all,
and which, upon no sort of urgent reason at the
time, they were deprived of? If such means can
with any probability be shown, from circumstances,
rather to add strength to our mixed ecclesiastical
and secular constitution, than to weaken it, surely
they are means infinitely to be preferred to penalties,
incapacities, and proscriptions continued from generation to generation. They are perfectly consistent
with the other parts of the coronation oath, in which
the king swears to maintain " the laws of God and
the true profession of the Gospel, and to govern the
people according to the statutes in Parliament
agreed upon, and the laws and customs of the
realm."   In consenting to such a statute, the Crown
would act at least as agreeable to the laws of God,
and to the true profession of the Gospel, and to the
laws and customs of the kingdom, as George I. did
when he passed the statute which took from the
body of the people everything which to that hour,
and even after the monstrous Acts of the 2nd and

8th of Anne (the objects of our common hatred), they still enjoyed inviolate.

It is hard to distinguish with the last degree of accuracy what laws are fundamental and what not. However, there is a distinction between them authorized by the writers on jurisprudence, and recognized in some of our statutes. I admit the Acts of King William and Queen Anne to be fundamental, but they are not the only fundamental laws. The law called Magna Charta, by which it is provided that " no man shall be disseized of his liberties and free customs but by the judgment of his peers, or the laws of the land" (meaning clearly for some proved crime tried and adjudged), I take to be a fundamental law. Now, although this Magna Charta, or some of the statutes establishing it, provide that that law shall be perpetual, and all statutes contrary to it shall be void, yet I cannot go so far as to deny the authority of statutes made in defiance of Magna Charta and all its principles. This, however, I will say, that it is a very venerable law, made by very wise and learned men, and that the Legislature, in their attempt to perpetuate it, even against the authority of future Parliaments, have shown their judgment that it is fundamental, on the same grounds and in the same manner that the Act of the 5th of Anne has considered and declared the establishment of the Church of England to be fundamental. Magna Charta, which secured these franchises to the subjects, regarded the rights of freeholders in counties to be as much a fundamental part of the Constitution as the establishment of the Church of England was thought, either at that time, or in the Act of King William, or in the Act of Queen Anne.

The Churchmen who led in that transaction certainly took care of the material interest of which they were the natural guardians. It is the first article of Magna Charta "that the Church of England shall be free," &c. &c. But at that period Churchmen, and barons, and knights, took care of the franchises and free customs of the people too. Those franchises are part of the Constitution itself, and inseparable from it. It would be a very strange thing if there should not only exist anomalies in our laws, a thing not easy to prevent, but that the fundamental parts of the Constitution should be perpetually and irreconcilably at variance with each other. I cannot persuade myself that the lovers of our Church are not as able to find effectual ways of reconciling its safety with the franchises of the people, as the ecclesiastics of the thirteenth century were able to do ; I cannot conceive how anything worse can be said of the Protestant religion of the Church of England than this, that wherever it is judged proper to give it a legal establishment, it becomes necessary to deprive the body of the people, if they adhere to their old opinions, of "their liberties and of all their free customs," and to reduce them to a state of civil servitude.

There is no man on earth, I believe, more willing than I am to lay it down as a fundamental of the Constitution, that the Church of England should be united and even identified with it; but allowing this, I cannot allow that all laws of regulation, made from time to time, in support of that fundamental law, are of course equally fundamental and equally unchangeable. This would be to confound all the branches of legislation and of jurisprudence. The crown and the personal safety of the monarch are fundamentals in our Constitution; yet I hope that no man regrets that the rabble of statutes got together during the reign of Henry the Eighth, by which treasons are multiplied with so prolific an energy, have been all repealed in a body; although they were all, or most of them, made in support of things truly fundamental in our Constitution. So were several of the Acts by which the Crown exercised its supremacy; such as the Act of Elizabeth, for making the high commission courts, and the like; as well as things made treason in the time of Charles II. None of this species of secondary and subsidiary laws have been held fundamental. They have yielded to circumstances, particularly where they were thought, even in their consequences, or obliquely, to affect other fundamentals. How much more certainly ought they to give way when, as in our case, they affect,

not here and there, in some particular point, or in
their consequence, but universally, collectively, and
directly, the fundamental franchises of a people,
equal to the whole inhabitants of several respectable
kingdoms and states—equal to the subjects of the
kings of Sardinia or of Denmark, equal to those of
the United Netherlands, and more than are to be
found in all the States of Switzerland. This way of
proscribing men by whole nations, as it were, from
all the benefits of the Constitution to which they
were born, I never can believe to be politic or
expedient, much less necessary for the existence of
any State or Church in the world. Whenever I
shall be convinced, which will be late and reluctantly,
that the safety of the Church is utterly inconsistent
with all the civil rights whatsoever of the far larger
part of the inhabitants of our country, I shall be extremely sorry for it; because I shall think the
Church to be truly in danger. It is putting things
into the position of an ugly alternative, into which,
I hope in God, they never will be put.

I have said most of what occurs to me on the
topics you touch upon, relative to the religion of the
king and his coronation oath. I shall conclude the
observations which I wished to submit to you on
this point, by assuring you that I think you the
most remote that can be conceived from the meta-
physicians of our times, who are the most foolish of
men, and who, dealing in universals and essences, see

no difference between more and less ; and who of course would think that the reason of the law which obliged the king to be a communicant of the Church of England would be as valid to exclude a Catholic from being an exciseman, or to deprive a man who has five hundred a year, under that description, from voting on a par with a factitious Protestant dissenting freeholder of forty shillings.

Recollect, my dear friend, that it was a fundamental principle in the French monarchy, whilst it stood, that the State should be Catholic ; yet the Edict of Nantz gave, not a full ecclesiastical, but a complete civil establishment, with places of which only they were capable, to the Calvinists of France ; and there were very few employments indeed of which they were not capable. The world praised the Cardinal de Richelieu, who took the first opportunity to strip them of their fortified places and cautionary towns. The same world held and does hold in execration (so far as that business is concerned) the memory of Louis the Fourteenth, for the total repeal of that favourable edict ; though the talk of " fundamental laws, established religion, religion of the prince, safety to the State," &c. &c., was then as largely held, and with as bitter a revival of the animosities of the civil confusions during the struggles between the parties, as now they can be in Ireland.

Perhaps there are persons who think that the same reason does not hold when the religious relation of the sovereign and subject is changed ; but they who have their shop full of false weights and measures, and who imagine that the adding or taking away the name of Protestant or Papist, Guelph or Ghibelline, alters all the principles of equity, policy, and prudence, leave us no common data upon which we can reason. I therefore pass by all this, which on you will make no impression, to come to what seems to be a serious consideration in your mind ; I mean the dread you express of "reviewing, for the purpose of altering, the principles of the Revolution." This is an interesting topic, on which I will, as fully as your leisure and mine permits, lay before you the ideas I have formed.

First, I cannot possibly confound in my mind all the things which were done at the Revolution with the principles of the Revolution. As in most great changes, many things were done from the necessities of the time, well or ill understood, from passion or from vengeance, which were not only not perfectly agreeable to its principles, but in the most direct contradiction to them. I shall not think that the deprivation of some millions of people of all the rights of citizens, and all interest in the Constitution in and to which they were born, was a thing conformable to the declared principles of the Revolution. This I am sure is true relatively to England (where the operation of these anti-principles comparatively were of little extent), and some of our

late laws, in repealing Acts made immediately after
the Revolution, admit that some things then done
were not done in the true spirit of the Revolution.
But the Revolution operated differently in England
and Ireland, in many, and these essential particulars.
Supposing the principles to have been altogether
the same in both kingdoms, by the application of
those principles to very different objects, the whole
spirit of the system was changed, not to say reversed.
In England it was the struggle of the great body
of the people for the establishment of their liberties,
against the efforts of a very small faction, who
would have oppressed them. In Ireland it was the
establishment of the power of the smaller number
at the expense of the civil liberties and properties
of the far greater part, and at the expense of the
political liberties of the whole. It was, to say the
truth, not a revolution, but a conquest; which is
not to say a great deal in its favour. To insist on
everything done in Ireland at the Revolution would
be to insist on the severe and jealous policy of a
conqueror, in the crude settlement of his new acquisition, as a permanent rule for its future government.
This, no power, in no country that ever I heard of,
has done or professed to do—except in Ireland;
where it is done, and possibly by some people will
be professed. Time has, by degrees, in all other
places and periods, blended and coalited the conquered with the conquerors. So, after some time,

and after one of the most rigid conquests that we
read of in history, the Normans softened into the
English.   I wish you to turn your recollection to
the fine speech of Cerealis to the Gauls, made to
dissuade them from revolt.   Speaking of the
Romans—" Nos   quamvis   toties   lacessiti,   jure
victoriæ id solum vobis addidimus, quo pacem
tueremur ; nam neque quies gentium sine armis ;
neque arma sine stipendiis ; neque stipendia sine
tributis, haberi queant.   Cætera in communi sita
sunt : ipsi plerumque nostris exercitibus præsidetis :
ipsi has aliasque provincias regitis : nil seperatum
clausumve—Proinde pacem et urbem, quam victores
victique eodem jure obtinemus, amate, colite."   You
will consider whether the arguments used by that
Roman to these Gauls would apply to the case in
Ireland ; and whether you could use so plausible a
preamble to any severe warning you might think it
proper to hold out to those who should resort to
sedition instead of supplication, to obtain any
object that they may pursue with the governing
power.

For a much longer period than that which had
sufficed to blend the Romans with the nation to
which of all others they were the most adverse, the
Protestants settled in Ireland, considered themselves
in no other light than that of a sort of a colonial
garrison, to keep the natives in subjection to the
other State of Great Britain.   The whole spirit of

the revolution in Ireland was that of not the mildest conqueror. In truth, the spirit of those proceedings did not commence at that era, nor was religion of any kind their primary object. What was done was not in the spirit of a contest between two religious factions, but between two adverse nations. The Statutes of Kilkenny show that the spirit of the Popery laws, and some even of their actual provisions, as applied between Englishry and Irishry, had existed in that harassed country before the words Protestant and Papist were heard of in the world. If we read Baron Finglas, Spenser, and Sir John Davis, we cannot miss the true genius and policy of the English Government there before the Revolution, as well as during the whole reign of Queen Elizabeth. Sir John Davis boasts of the benefits received by the natives, by extending to them the English law and turning the whole kingdom into shire ground. But the appearance of things alone was changed. The original scheme was never deviated from for a single hour. Unheard-of confiscations were made in the northern parts, upon grounds of plots and conspiracies, never proved upon their supposed authors. The war of chicane succeeded to the war of arms and of hostile statutes ; and a regular series of operations were carried on, particularly from Chichester's time, in the ordinary courts of justice and by special commissions and inquisitions ; first,

under pretence of tenures, and then of titles in the
Crown, for the purpose of the total extirpation of the
interest of the natives in their own soil—until this
species of subtle ravage, being carried to the last
excess of oppression and insolence under Lord
Strafford, it kindled the flames of that rebellion
which broke out in 1641. By the issue of that war,
by the turn which the Earl of Clarendon gave to
things at the Restoration, and by the total reduction
of the kingdom of Ireland in 1691, the ruin of the
native Irish, and in a great measure, too, of the first
races of the English, was completely accomplished.
The new English interest was settled with as solid a
stability as anything in human affairs can look for.
All the penal laws of that unparalleled code of
oppression, which were made after the last event,
were manifestly the effects of national hatred and
scorn towards a conquered people, whom the victors
delighted to trample upon, and were not at all afraid
to provoke.   They were not the effect of their fears,
but of their security. They who carried on this
system looked to the irresistible force of Great
Britain for their support in their acts of power.
They were quite certain that no complaints of the
natives would be heard on this side of the water
with any other sentiments than those of contempt
and indignation.   Their cries served only to augment
their torture. Machines which could answer their
purposes so well must be of an excellent contrivance.

Indeed, in England the double name of the com-
plainants, Irish and Papists (it would be hard to say,
singly, which singly was the most odious) shut up
the hearts of every one against them. Whilst that
temper prevailed, and it prevailed in all its force to
a time within our memory, every measure was
pleasing and popular just in proportion as it tended
to harass and ruin a set of people who were looked
upon as enemies to God and man ; and indeed as a
race of bigoted savages who were a disgrace to
human nature itself.

However, as the English in Ireland began to be
domiciliated, they began also to recollect that they
had a country. The English interest, at first by
faint and almost insensible degrees, but at length
openly and avowedly, became an independent Irish
interest ; full as independent as it could ever have
been if it had continued in the persons of the native
Irish ; and it was maintained with more skill and
more consistency than probably it would have been in
theirs. With their views the Anglo-Irish changed
their maxims—it was necessary to demonstrate to
the whole people that there was something at least
of a common interest, combined with the indepen-
dency, which was to become the object of common
exertions. The mildness of government produced
the first relaxation towards the Irish ; the necessities
and, in part too, the temper that predominated at
this great change, produced the second and the most

important of these relaxations. English Government and Irish Legislature felt jointly the propriety of this measure. The Irish Parliament and nation became independent.

The true revolution to you, that which most intrinsically and substantially resembled the English revolution of 1688, was the Irish revolution of 1782. The Irish Parliament of 1782 bore little resemblance to that which sat in that kingdom after the period of the first of these revolutions. It bore a much nearer resemblance to that which sat under King James. The change of the Parliament in 1782 from the character of the Parliament which, as a token of its indignation, had burned all the journals indiscriminately of the former Parliament in the council chamber, was very visible. The address of King William's Parliament, the Parliament which assembled after the Revolution, amongst other causes of complaint (many of them sufficiently just), complains of the repeal by their predecessors of Poyning's law—no absolute idol with the Parliament of 1782.

Great Britain finding the Anglo-Irish highly animated with a spirit, which had indeed shown itself before, though with little energy and many interruptions, and therefore suffered a multitude of uniform precedents to be established against it, acted in my opinion with the greatest temperance and wisdom. She saw that the disposition of the leading part of the nation would not permit them to act any

longer the part of a garrison. She saw that true
policy did not require that they ever should have
appeared in that character; or if it had done so
formerly, the reasons had now ceased to operate.
She saw that the Irish of her race were resolved to
build their Constitution and their politics upon
another bottom. With those things under her view,
she instantly complied with the whole of your
demands, without any reservation whatsoever. She
surrendered that boundless superiority for the preservation of which, and the acquisition, she had supported the English colonies in Ireland for so long
a time, and at so vast an expense (according to the
standard of those ages) of her blood and treasure.

When we bring before us the matter which history
affords for our selection, it is not improper to
examine the spirit of the several precedents which
are candidates for our choice. Might it not be as
well for your statesmen on the other side of the
water, to take an example from this latter, and surely
more conciliatory revolution, as a pattern for your
conduct towards your own fellow-citizens, than from
that of 1688, when a paramount sovereignty over
both you and them was more loftily claimed, and
more sternly exerted, than at any former or at any
subsequent period? Great Britain in 1782 rose
above the vulgar ideas of policy, the ordinary
jealousies of State, and all the sentiments of national
pride and national ambition. If she had been more

disposed than, I thank God for it, she was, to listen
to the suggestions of passion, than to the dictates of
prudence, she might have urged the principles, the
maxims, the policy, the practice of the Revolution,
against the demands of the leading description in
Ireland, with full as much plausibility, and full as
good a grace, as any amongst them can possibly do,
against the supplications of so vast and extensive a
description of their own people.

A good deal too, if the spirit of domination and
exclusion had prevailed in England, might have been
excepted against some of the means then employed
in Ireland, whilst her claims were in agitation.
They were at least as much out of ordinary course
as those which are now objected against admitting
your people to any of the benefits of an English
Constitution.   Most certainly, neither with you, nor
here, was any one ignorant of what was at that time
said, written, and done. But on all sides we
separated the means from the end ; and we separated
the cause of the moderate and rational from the ill-
intentioned and seditious, which on such occasions
are so frequently apt to march together.   At that
time, on your part, you were not afraid to review
what was done at the revolution of 1688 ; and what
had been continued during the subsequent flourishing
period of the British empire. The change then made
was a great and fundamental alteration. In the execution, it was an operose business on both sides of the

water. It required the repeal of several laws, the modification of many, and a new course to be given to an infinite number of legislative, judicial, and official practices and usages in both kingdoms. This did not frighten any of us. You are now asked to give, in some moderate measure, to your fellow-citizens, what Great Britain gave to you without any measure at all. Yet, notwithstanding all the difficulties at the time, and the apprehensions which some very well-meaning people entertained, through the admirable temper in which this revolution (or restoration in the nature of a revolution) was conducted in both kingdoms, it has hitherto produced no inconvenience to either ; and I trust, with the continuance of the same temper, that it never will. I think that this small, inconsiderable change relative to an exclusive statute not made at the Revolution for restoring the people to the benefits, from which the green soreness of a civil war had not excluded them, will be productive of no sort of mischief whatsoever. Compare what was done in 1782 with what is wished in 1792 ; consider the spirit of what has been done at the several periods of reformation ; and weigh maturely whether it be exactly true that conciliatory concessions are of good policy only in discussions between nations ; but that among descriptions in the same nation they must always be irrational and dangerous. What have you suffered in your peace, your prosperity, or, in what ought ever to be dear to a nation, your glory, by the last act by which you took the property of that people under the protection of the laws? What reason have you to dread the consequences of admitting the people possessing that property to some share in the protection of the Constitution?

I do not mean to trouble you with anything to remove the objections—I will not call them arguments—against this measure, taken from a ferocious hatred to all that numerous description of Christians. It would be to pay a poor compliment to your understanding or your heart. Neither your religion nor your politics consist "in odd, perverse antipathies." You are not resolved to persevere in proscribing from the Constitution so many millions of your countrymen, because, in contradiction to experience and to common sense, you think proper to imagine that their principles are subversive of common human society. To that I shall only say, that whoever has a temper which can be gratified by indulging himself in these good-natured fancies, ought to do a great deal more. For an exclusion from the privileges of British subjects is not a cure for so terrible a distemper of the human mind, as they are pleased to suppose in their countrymen. I rather conceive a participation in those privileges to be itself a remedy for some mental disorders.

As little shall I detain you with matters that can as little obtain admission into a mind like yours;

such as the fear, or pretence of fear, that, in spite of
your own power, and the trifling power of Great
Britain, you may be conquered by the Pope ; or that
this commodious bugbear (who is of infinitely more
use to those who pretend to fear, than to those who
love him) will absolve his Majesty's subjects from
their allegiance, and send over the Cardinal of York
to rule you as his viceroy ; or that, by the plenitude
of his power, he will take that fierce tyrant, the King
of the French, out of his jail, and arm that nation
(which on all occasions treats his Holiness so very
politely) with his bulls and pardons, to invade poor
old Ireland, to reduce you to popery and slavery,
and to force the free-born, naked feet of your people
into the wooden shoes of that arbitrary monarch. I
do not believe that discourses of this kind are held,
or that anything like them will be held, by any who
walk about without a keeper. Yet I confess that
on occasions of this nature I am the most afraid of
the weakest reasonings, because they discover the
strongest passions. These things will never be
brought out in definite propositions. They would
not prevent pity towards any persons, they would
only cause it for those who were capable of talking
in such a strain. But I know, and am sure, that
such ideas as no man will distinctly produce to
another, or hardly venture to bring in any plain
shape to his own mind, he will utter in obscure,
ill-explained doubts, jealousies, surmises, fears, and

apprehensions; and that in such a fog they will appear to have a good deal of size, and will make an impression ; when, if they were clearly brought forth and defined, they would meet with nothing but scorn and derision.

There is another way of taking an objection to this concession, which I admit to be something more plausible, and worthy of a more attentive examination. It is, that this numerous class of people is mutinous, disorderly, prone to sedition, and easy to be wrought upon by the insidious arts of wicked and designing men ; that, conscious of this, the sober, rational, and wealthy part of that body, who are totally of another character, do by no means desire any participation for themselves, or for any one else of their description, in the franchises of the British Constitution.

I have great doubt of the exactness of any part of this observation. But let us admit that the body of the Catholics are prone to sedition (of which, as I have said, I entertain much doubt), is it possible, that any fair observer or fair reasoner can think of confining this description to them only ? I believe it to be possible for men to be mutinous and seditious who feel no grievance ; but I believe no man will assert seriously, that when people are of a turbulent spirit, the best way to keep them in order is to furnish them with something substantial to complain of.

You separate very properly the sober, rational, and substantial part of their description from the rest. You give, as you ought to do, weight only to the former. What I have always thought of the matter is this—that the most poor, illiterate, and uninformed creatures upon earth, are judges of a practical oppression. It is a matter of feeling, and as such persons generally have felt most of it, and are not of an over-lively sensibility, they are the best judges of it. But for the real cause, or the appropriate remedy, they ought never to be called into council about the one or the other. They ought to be totally shut out, because their reason is weak, because when once roused, their passions are ungoverned, because they want information, because the smallness of the property which individually they possess, renders them less attentive to the consequence of the measures they adopt in affairs of moment. When I find a great cry amongst the people, who speculate little, I think myself called seriously to examine into it, and to separate the real cause from the ill effects of the passion it may excite, and the bad use which artful men may make of an irritation of the popular mind. Here we must be aided by persons of a contrary character; we must not listen to the desperate or the furious ; but it is therefore necessary for us to distinguish who are the really indigent, and the really intemperate. As to the persons who desire this part in

the Constitution, I have no reason to imagine that
they are men who have nothing to lose and much
to look for in public confusion. The popular
meeting, from which apprehensions have been
entertained, has assembled. I have accidentally
had conversation with two friends of mine, who
know something of the gentleman who was put
into the chair upon that occasion : one of them
has had money transactions with him ; the other,
from curiosity, has been to see his concerns. They
both tell me he is a man of some property, but
you must be the best judge of this, who, by your
office, are likely to know his transactions. Many
of the others are certainly persons of fortune ; and
all, or most, fathers of families, men in respectable
ways of life, and some of them far from contemptible,
either for their information, or for the abilities which
they have shown in the discussion of their interests.
What such men think it for their advantage to
acquire, ought not, *primâ facie*, to be considered as
rash or heady, or incompatible with the public
safety or welfare.

I admit that men of the best fortunes and repu-
tations, and of the best talents and education too,
may by accident show themselves furious and intemperate in their desires. This is a great misfortune when it happens ; for the first presumptions
are undoubtedly in their favour. We have two
standards of judging in this case of the sanity and

sobriety of any proceedings, of unequal certainty indeed, but neither of them to be neglected : the first is by the value of the object sought, the next is by the means through which it is pursued.

The object pursued by the Catholics is, I understand, and have all along reasoned as if it were so, in some degree or measure to be again admitted to the franchises of the Constitution. Men are considered as under some derangement of their intellects when they see good and evil in a different light from other men, when they choose nauseous and unwholesome food, and reject such as to the rest of the world seems pleasant and is known to be nutritive. I have always considered the British Constitution not to be a thing in itself so vicious as that none but men of deranged understanding and turbulent tempers could desire a share in it ; on the contrary, I should think very indifferently of the understanding and temper of any body of men who did not wish to partake of this great and acknowledged benefit. I cannot think quite so favourably either of the sense or temper of those, if any such there are, who would voluntarily persuade their brethren that the object is not fit for them or they for the object. Whatever may be my thoughts concerning them, I am quite sure that they who hold such language must forfeit all credit with the rest. This is infallible. If they conceive any opinion of their judgment they cannot possibly

think them their friends. There is, indeed, one
supposition which would reconcile the conduct of
such gentlemen to sound reason, and to the purest
affection towards their fellow-sufferers; it is that
they act under the impression of a well-grounded
fear for the general interest. If they should be
told, and should believe the story, that if they dare
attempt to make their condition better they will
infallibly make it worse; that if they aim at
obtaining liberty they will have their slavery
doubled; that their endeavour to put themselves
upon anything which approaches towards an equitable footing with their fellow-subjects, will be considered as an indication of a seditious and rebellious
disposition; such a view of things ought perfectly
to restore the gentlemen, who so anxiously dissuade their countrymen from wishing a participation with the privileged part of the people, to the
good opinion of their fellows. But what is to them
a very full justification is not quite so honourable
to that power from whose maxims and temper so
good a ground of rational terror is furnished. I
think arguments of this kind will never be used by
the friends of a Government which I greatly respect;
or by any of the leaders of an Opposition whom I
have the honour to know and the sense to admire.
I remember Polybius tells us, that during his captivity
in Italy as a Peloponnesian hostage, he solicited old
Cato to intercede with the Senate for his release

and that of his countrymen ; this old politician told
him that he had better continue in his present condition, however irksome, than apply again to that
formidable authority for their relief; that he ought
to imitate the wisdom of his countryman Ulysses,
who, when he was once out of the den of the Cyclops,
had too much sense to venture again into the same
cavern. But I conceive too high an opinion of the
Irish Legislature to think that they are to their fellow-
citizens what the grand oppressors of mankind were
to a people whom the fortune of war had subjected
to their power. For though Cato could use such a
parallel with regard to his Senate, I should really
think it nothing short of impious to compare an
Irish Parliament to a den of Cyclops. I hope the
people, both here and with you, will always apply
to the House of Commons with becoming modesty,
but at the same time with minds unembarrassed with
any sort of terror.

As to the means which the Catholics employ to
obtain this object, so worthy of sober and rational
minds, I do admit that such means may be used in
the pursuit of it as may make it proper for the Legislature in this case to defer their compliance until
the demandants are brought to a proper sense of
their duty. A concession in which the governing
power of our country loses its dignity is dearly
bought even by him who obtains his object. All
the people have a deep interest in the dignity of

I 2

Parliament.   But, as the refusal of franchises which
are drawn out of the first vital stamina of the British
Constitution is a very serious thing, we ought to be
very sure that the manner and spirit of the application is offensive and dangerous indeed, before we
ultimately reject all applications of this nature.   The
mode of application, I hear, is by petition.   It is
the manner in which all the sovereign powers of the
world are approached, and I never heard (except in
the case of James the Second) that any prince considered this manner of supplication to be contrary to
the humility of a subject, or to the respect due to
the person or authority of the sovereign.   This rule
and a correspondent practice are observed from the
Grand Seignior down to the most petty prince or
republic in Europe.

   You have sent me several papers, some in print,
some in manuscript.   I think I had seen all of them,
except the formula of association.   I confess they
appear to me to contain matter mischievous and
capable of giving alarm, if the spirit in which they
are written should be found to make any considerable
progress.   But I am at a loss to know how to apply
them as objections to the case now before us.   When
I find that the general committee which acts for the
Roman Catholics in Dublin prefers the association
proposed in the written draft you have sent me, to
a respectful application in Parliament, I shall think
the persons who sign such a paper to be unworthy

of any privilege which may be thought fit to be granted ; and that such men ought, by name, to be excepted from any benefit under the Constitution to which they offer this violence. But I do not find that this form of a seditious league has been signed by any person whatsoever, either on the part of the supposed projectors, or on the part of those whom it is calculated to seduce. I do not find, on inquiry, that such a thing was mentioned, or even remotely alluded to, in the general meeting of the Catholics, from which so much violence was apprehended. I have considered the other publications, signed by individuals on the part of certain societies : I may mistake, for I have not the honour of knowing them personally, but I take Mr. Butler and Mr. Tandy not to be Catholics, but members of the Established Church. Not one that I recollect of these publica-tions, which you and I equally dislike, appears to be written by persons of that persuasion. Now, if, whilst a man is dutifully soliciting a favour from Parliament, any person should choose, in an improper manner, to show his inclination towards the cause depending, and if that must destroy the cause of the petitioner, then not only the petitioner, but the Legislature itself, is in the power of any weak friend or artful enemy that the supplicant or that the Par-liament may have. A man must be judged by his own actions only. Certain Protestant Dissenters make seditious propositions to the Catholics, which it does not appear that they have yet accepted.   It would be strange that the tempter should escape all punishment, and that he who, under circumstances full of seduction and full of provocation, has resisted the temptation, should incur the penalty.   You know that, with regard to the Dissenters, who are stated to be the chief movers in this vile scheme of altering the principles of election to a right of voting by the head, you are not able (if you ought even to wish such a thing) to deprive them of any part of the franchises and privileges which they hold on a footing of perfect equality with yourselves.   They may do what they please with constitutional impunity, but the others cannot even listen with civility to an invitation from them to an ill-judged scheme of liberty, without forfeiting for ever all hopes of any of those liberties which we admit to be sober and rational.

It is known, I believe, that the greater as well as the sounder part of our excluded countrymen, have not adopted the wild ideas, and wilder engagements, which have been held out to them ; but have rather chosen to hope small and safe concessions from the legal power, than boundless objects from trouble and confusion.   This mode of action seems to me to mark men of sobriety, and to distinguish them from those who are intemperate from circumstance or from nature.   But why do they not instantly disclaim and disavow those who make such advances to them? In this too, in my opinion, they show themselves no less sober and circumspect. In the present moment, nothing short of insanity could induce them to take such a step. Pray consider the circumstances. Disclaim, says somebody, all union with the Dissenters. Right; but when this your injunction is obeyed, shall I obtain the object which I solicit from you? Oh, no, nothing at all like it! But in punishing us by an exclusion from the Constitution through the great gate, for having been invited to enter into it by a postern, will you punish by deprivation of their privileges, or mulct in any other way, those who have tempted us? Far from it; we mean to preserve all their liberties and immunities, as our life-blood. We mean to cultivate them, as brethren whom we love and respect; with you we have no fellowship. We can bear with patience their enmity to ourselves; but their friendship with you we will not endure. But mark it well! All our quarrels with them are always to be revenged upon you. Formerly, it is notorious that we should have resented with the highest indignation your presuming to show any ill-will to them. You must not suffer them now to show any goodwill to you. Know—and take it once for all—that it is, and ever has been, and ever will be, a fundamental maxim in our politics, that you are not to have any part, or shadow, or name of interest whatever in our State. That we look upon you as

under an irreversible outlawry from our Constitution
—as perpetual and unalliable aliens.

Such, my dear Sir, is the plain nature of the argument drawn from the Revolution maxims, enforced
by a supposed disposition in the Catholics to unite
with the Dissenters.   Such it is, though it were
clothed in never such bland and civil forms, and
wrapped up, as a poet says, in a thousand "artful
folds of sacred lawn."   For my own part, I do not
know in what manner to shape such arguments so
as to obtain admission for them into a rational
understanding.   Everything of this kind is to be
reduced at last to threats of power.   I cannot say
væ victis, and then throw the sword into the scale.   I
have no sword; and if I had, in this case most
certainly I would not use it as a make-weight in
political reasoning.

Observe, on these principles, the difference between
the procedure of the Parliament and the Dissenters
towards the people in question.   One employs
courtship, the other force.   The Dissenters offer
bribes ; the Parliament nothing but the *front negatif*
of a stern and forbidding authority.   A man may be
very wrong in his ideas of what is good for him.
But no man affronts me, nor can therefore justify my
affronting him, by offering to make me as happy as
himself, according to his own ideas of happiness.
This the Dissenters do to the Catholics.   You are on
the different extremes.   The Dissenters offer, with

regard to constitutional rights and civil advantages of
all sorts, everything ; you refuse everything. With
them there is boundless though not very assured
hope ; with you, a very sure and very unqualified
despair.   The terms of alliance from the Dissenters
offer a representation of the Commons, chosen out of
the people by the head.   This is absurdly and
dangerously large in my opinion ; and that scheme
of election is known to have been, at all times,
perfectly odious to me.   But I cannot think it right,
of course, to punish the Irish Roman Catholics by a
universal exclusion, because others, whom you would
not punish at all, propose a universal admission.   I
cannot dissemble to myself, that in this very kingdom
many persons, who are not in the situation of the
Irish Catholics, but who, on the contrary, enjoy the
full benefit of the Constitution as it stands, and some
of whom, from the effect of their fortunes, enjoy it in
a large measure, had some years ago associated to
procure great and undefined changes (they considered
them as reforms) in the popular part of the Constitution.   Our friend the late Mr. Flood (no slight man)
proposed in his place, and in my hearing, a representation not much less extensive than this, for England ;
in which every house was to be inhabited by a voter
—in addition to all the actual votes by other titles
(some of the corporate) which we know do not require
a house or a shed.   Can I forget that a person of the
very highest rank, of very large fortune, and of the

first class of ability, brought a Bill into the House of
Lords, in the headquarters of aristocracy, containing
identically the same project for the supposed adoption of which by a club or two it is thought right to
extinguish all hopes in the Roman Catholics of
Ireland ?   I cannot say it was very eagerly embraced
or very warmly pursued.   But the Lords neither did
disavow the Bill, nor treat it with any disregard; nor
express any sort of disapprobation of its noble
author, who has never lost, with king or people, the
least degree of the respect and consideration which
so justly belongs to him.

I am not at all enamoured, as I have told you, with
this plan of representation ; as little do I relish any
bandings or associations for procuring it.   But if the
question was to be put to you and me—universal
popular representation, or none at all for us and ours
—we should find ourselves in a very awkward
position.   I do not like this kind of dilemmas,
especially when they are practical.

Then, since our oldest fundamental laws follow,
or rather couple, freehold with franchise ; since no
principle of the Revolution shakes these liberties ;
since the oldest and one of the best monuments of
the Constitution demands for the Irish the privilege
which they supplicate ; since the principles of the
Revolution coincide with the declarations of the Great
Charter ; since the practice of the Revolution, in this
point, did not contradict its principles ; since, from

that event, twenty-five years had elapsed before a
domineering party, on a party principle, had ventured
to disfranchise, without any proof whatsoever of abuse,
the greater part of the community ; since the king's
coronation oath does not stand in his way to the
performance of his duty to all his subjects ; since
you have given to all other Dissenters these privileges without limit, which are hitherto withheld,
without any limitation whatsoever, from the
Catholics ; since no nation in the world has ever
been known to exclude so great a body of men
(not born slaves) from the civil State, and all the
benefits of its Constitution ; the whole question
comes before Parliament as a matter for its
prudence. I do not put the thing on a question of
right. That discretion which in judicature is well
said by Lord Coke to be a crooked cord, in legislature is a golden rule. Supplicants ought not to
appear too much in the character of litigants. If
the subject thinks so highly and reverently of the
sovereign authority, as not to claim anything of right,
so that it may seem to be independent of the power
and free choice of its government ; and if the
sovereign, on his part, considers the advantages of
the subjects as their right, and all their reasonable
wishes as so many claims ; in the fortunate con-
junction of these mutual dispositions are laid the
foundations of a happy and prosperous commonwealth. For my own part, desiring of all things

that the authority of the Legislature under which I
was born, and which I cherish, not only with a
dutiful awe, but with a partial and cordial affection,
to be maintained in the utmost possible respect, I
never will suffer myself to suppose that at bottom
their discretion will be found to be at variance with
their justice.

The whole being at discretion, I beg leave just
to suggest some matters for your consideration :
whether the government in Church or State is likely
to be more secure by continuing causes of grounded
discontent, to a very great number (say two millions)
of the subjects ? or, whether the Constitution, combined and balanced as it is, will be rendered more
solid by depriving so large a part of the people of
all concern, or interest, or share in its representation,
actual or virtual ?   I here mean to lay an emphasis
on the word virtual.   Virtual representation is that
in which there is a communion of interests and a
sympathy in feelings and desires between those who
act in the name of any description of people and
the people in whose name they act, though the
trustees are not actually chosen by them.   This is
virtual representation.   Such a representation I
think to be, in many cases, even better than the
actual.   It possesses most of its advantages, and
is free from many of its inconveniences ; it corrects
the irregularities in the literal representation, when
the shifting current of human affairs, or the acting

of public interests in different ways, carry it obliquely
from its first line of direction. The people may
err in their choice; but common interest and
common sentiment are rarely mistaken. But this
sort of virtual representation cannot have a long or
sure existence, if it has not a substratum in the
actual. The member must have some relation to
the constituent. As things stand, the Catholic,
as a Catholic and belonging to a description, has
no virtual relation to the representative; but the
contrary. There is a relation in mutual obligation. Gratitude may not always have a very
lasting power; but the frequent recurrence of an
application for favours will revive and refresh it,
and will necessarily produce some degree of mutual
attention. It will produce, at least, acquaintance.
The several descriptions of people will not be kept
so much apart as they now are, as if they were not
only separate nations, but separate species. The
stigma and reproach, the hideous mask, will be taken
off, and men will see each other as they are. Sure
I am that there have been thousands in Ireland
who have never conversed with a Roman Catholic
in their whole lives, unless they happened to talk to
their gardener's workmen, or to ask their way, when
they had lost it, in their sports; or, at best, who had
known them only as footmen, or other domestics of
the second and third order; and so averse were they
some time ago to have them near their persons, that

they would not employ even those who could never find their way beyond the stable. I well remember a great and in many respects a good man, who advertised for a blacksmith, but at the same time added he must be a Protestant. It is impossible that such a state of things, though natural goodness in many persons will undoubtedly make exceptions, must not produce alienation on the one side, and pride and insolence on the other.

Reduced to a question of discretion, and that discretion exercised solely upon what will appear best for the conservation of the State on its present basis, I should recommend it to your serious thoughts, whether the narrowing of the foundation is always the best way to secure the building? The body of disfranchised men will not be perfectly satisfied to remain always in that state. If they are not satisfied you have two millions of subjects in your bosom, full of uneasiness ; not that they cannot overturn the Act of Settlement, and put themselves and you under an arbitrary master ; or that they are not permitted to spawn an hydra of wild republics, on principles of a pretended natural equality in man ; but because you will not suffer them to enjoy the ancient, funda-mental, tried advantages of a British Constitution ; that you will not permit them to profit of the pro-tection of a common father, or the freedom of common citizens ; and that the only reason which can be assigned for this disfranchisement has a tendency more deeply to ulcerate their minds than the act of exclusion itself. What the consequence of such feelings must be, it is for you to look to. To warn is not to menace.

I am far from asserting that men will not excite disturbances without just cause. I know that such an assertion is not true. ; But neither is it true that disturbances have never just complaints for their origin. I am sure that it is hardly prudent to furnish them with such causes of complaint, as every man who thinks the British Constitution a benefit, may think, at least, colourable and plausible.

Several are in dread of the manœuvres of certain persons among the Dissenters, who turn this ill humour to their own ill purposes. You know, better than I can, how much these proceedings of certain among the Dissenters are to be feared. You are to weigh, with the temper which is natural to you, whether it may be for the safety of our establishment, that the Catholics should be ultimately persuaded that they have no hope to enter into the Constitution but through the Dissenters.

Think whether this be the way to prevent or dissolve factious combinations against the Church or the State. Reflect seriously on the possible consequences of keeping in the heart of your country a bank of discontent, every hour accumulating, upon which every description of seditious men may draw at pleasure. They whose principles of faction would

dispose them to the establishment of an arbitrary
monarchy, will find a nation of men who have no
sort of interest in freedom ; but who will have an
interest in that equality of justice or favour with
which a wise despot must view all his subjects who
do not attack the foundations of his power. Love
of liberty itself may, in such men, become the means
of establishing an arbitrary domination. On the
other hand, they who wish for a democratic republic
will find a set of men who have no choice between
civil servitude and the entire ruin of a mixed constitution.

Suppose the people of Ireland divided into three
parts ; of these (I speak within compass) two are
Catholic. Of the remaining third, one half is
composed of Dissenters. There is no natural union
between those descriptions. It may be produced.
If the two parts Catholic be driven into a close
confederacy with half the third part of Protestants,
with a view to a change in the constitution in
Church or State, or both, and you rest the whole of
their security on a handful of gentlemen, clergy, and
their dependants ; compute the strength you have
in Ireland to oppose to grounded discontent, to
capricious innovation, to blind popular fury, and to
ambitious turbulent intrigue.

You mention that the minds of some gentlemen
are a good deal heated ; and that it is often said
that, rather than submit to such persons having a

share in their franchises, they would throw up their independence, and precipitate a union with Great Britain. I have heard a discussion concerning such a union amongst all sorts of men ever since I remember anything. For my own part, I have never been able to bring my mind to anything clear and decisive upon the subject. There cannot be a more arduous question. As far as I can form an opinion, it would not be for the mutual advantage of the two kingdoms. Persons, however, more able than I am, think otherwise. But, whatever the merits of this union may be, to make it a menace, it must be shown to be an evil, and an evil more particularly to those who are threatened with it, than to those who hold it out as a terror. I really do not see how this threat of a union can operate, or that the Catholics are more likely to be losers by that measure than the Churchmen.

The humours of the people, and of politicians too, are so variable in themselves and are so much under the occasional influence of some leading men, that it is impossible to know what turn the public mind here would take on such an event. There is but one thing certain concerning it. Great divisions and vehement passions would precede this union, both on the measure itself and on its terms ; and particularly this very question of a share in the representation for the Catholics, from whence the project of a union originated, would form a principal part in the

discussion; and in the temper in which some
gentlemen seem inclined to throw themselves, by a
sort of high indignant passion, into the scheme, those
points would not be deliberated with all possible
calmness.

From my best observation I should greatly doubt
whether, in the end, these gentlemen would obtain
their object, so as to make the exclusion of two
millions of their countrymen a fundamental article in
the union. The demand would be of a nature quite
unprecedented. You might obtain the union ; and
yet a gentleman who, under the new union establishment, would aspire to the honour of representing his
county, might possibly be as much obliged, as he
may fear to be under the old separate establishment,
to the unsupportable mortification of asking his
neighbours, who have a different opinion concerning
the elements in the Sacrament, for their votes.

I believe, nay, I am sure, that the people of Great
Britain, with or without a union, might be depended
upon, in cases of any real danger, to aid the Government of Ireland with the same cordiality as they
would support their own against any wicked attempts
to shake the security of the happy constitution in
Church and State. But before Great Britain engages
in any quarrel, the cause of the dispute would certainly be a part of her consideration. If confusions
should arise in that kingdom, from too steady an
attachment to a proscriptive monopolizing system,

and from the resolution of regarding the franchise, and in it the security of the subject as belonging rather to religious opinions than to civil qualification and civil conduct, I doubt whether you might quite certainly reckon on obtaining an aid of force from hence for the support of that system. We might extend your distractions to this country by taking part in them. England will be indisposed, I suspect, to send an army for the conquest of Ireland. What was done in 1782 is a decisive proof of her sentiments of justice and moderation. She will not be fond of making another American war in Ireland. The principles of such a war would but too much resemble the former one. The well-disposed and the ill-disposed in England would (for different reasons perhaps) be equally averse to such an enterprise. The confiscations, the public auctions, the private grants, the plantations, the transplantations, which formerly animated so many adventurers, even among sober citizens, to such Irish expeditions, and which possibly might have animated some of them to the American, can have no existence in the case that we suppose.

Let us form a supposition (no foolish or ungrounded supposition) that in an age when men are infinitely more disposed to heat themselves with political than religious controversies, the former should entirely prevail, as we see that in some places they have prevailed over the latter, and that the

Catholics of Ireland, from the courtship paid them
on the one hand, and the high tone of refusal on
the other, should, in order to enter into all the
rights of subjects, all become Protestant Dissenters,
and, as the others do, take all your oaths. They
would all obtain their civil objects ; and the change,
for anything I know to the contrary (in the dark
as I am about the Protestant Dissenting tenets)
might be of use to the health of their souls. But
what security our constitution in Church or State
could derive from that event I cannot possibly
discern.   Depend upon it, it is as true as Nature
is true, that if you force them out of the religion
of habit, education, or opinion, it is not to yours
they will ever go.   Shaken in their minds, they
will go to that where the dogmas are fewest, where
they are the most uncertain, where they lead them
the least to a consideration of what they have
abandoned.   They will go to that uniformly democratic system to whose first movements they owed
their emancipation.   I recommend you seriously to
turn this in your mind.   Believe that it requires
your best and maturest thoughts.   Take what course
you please—union or no union ; whether the people
remain Catholics or become Protestant Dissenters,
sure it is that the present state of monopoly cannot
continue.

    If England were animated, as I think she is not,
with her former spirit of domination, and with the

strong theological hatred which she once cherished for that description of her fellow-Christians and fellow-subjects, I am yet convinced that, after the fullest success in a ruinous struggle, you would be obliged finally to abandon that monopoly. We were obliged to do this, even when everything promised success in the American business. If you should make this experiment at last, under the pressure of any necessity, you never can do it well. But if, instead of falling into a passion, the leading gentlemen of the country themselves should undertake the business cheerfully, and with hearty affection towards it, great advantages would follow. What is forced cannot be modified ; but here you may measure your concessions.

It is a consideration of great moment, that you may make the desired admission without altering the system of your representation in the smallest degree or in any part. You may leave that deliberation of a parliamentary change or reform, if ever you should think fit to engage in it, uncomplicated and unembarrassed with the other question. Whereas, if they are mixed and confounded, as some people attempt to mix and confound them, no one can answer for the effects on the Constitution itself.

There is another advantage in taking up this business singly and by an arrangement for the single object. It is, that you may proceed by degrees. We must all obey the great law of change. It is

the most powerful law of Nature, and the means
perhaps of its conservation. All we can do, and
that human wisdom can do, is to provide that the
change shall proceed by insensible degrees. This
has all the benefits which may be in change, without
any of the inconveniences of mutation. Everything
is provided for as it arrives. This mode will, on the
one hand, prevent the unfixing old interests at once ;
a thing which is apt to breed a black and sullen
discontent in those who are at once dispossessed of
all their influence and consideration. This gradual
course, on the other side, will prevent men, long
under depression, from being intoxicated with a large
draught of new power, which they always abuse
with a licentious insolence. But wishing, as I do,
the change to be gradual and cautious, I would in
my first steps lean rather to the side of enlargement
than restriction.

It is one excellence of our Constitution that all
our rights of provincial election regard rather
property than person. It is another that the rights
which approach more nearly to the personal are
most of them corporate, and suppose a restrained
and strict education of seven years in some useful
occupation. In both cases the practice may have
slid from the principle. The standard of qualification in both cases may be so low, or not so
judiciously chosen, as in some degree to frustrate
the end. But all this is for your prudence in the

case before you. You may rise a step or two the qualification of the Catholic voters. But if you were to-morrow to put the Catholic freeholder on the footing of the most favoured forty-shilling Protestant Dissenter, you know that, such is the actual state of Ireland, this would not make a sensible alteration in almost any'one election in the kingdom. The effect in their favour, even defensively, would be infinitely slow. But it would be healing ; it would be satisfactory and protecting. The stigma would be removed. By admitting settled permanent substance in lieu of the numbers, you would avoid the great danger of our time, that of setting up number against property. The numbers ought never to be neglected because (besides what is due to them as men) collectively, though not individually, they have great property : they ought to have therefore protection, they ought to have security, they ought to have even consideration ; but they ought not to predominate.

My dear Sir, I have nearly done. I meant to write you a long letter ; I have written a long dissertation. I might have done it earlier and better. I might have been more forcible and more clear, if I had not been interrupted as I have been ; and this obliges me not to write to you in my own hand. Though my hand but signs it, my heart goes with what I have written. Since I could think at all, those have been my thoughts. You know that thirty-two years ago they were as fully matured in my mind as they are now. A letter of mine to Lord Kenmare, though not by my desire, and full of lesser mistakes, has been printed in Dublin. It was written ten or twelve years ago, at the time when I began the employment, which I have not yet finished, in favour of another distressed people, injured by those who have vanquished them, or stolen a dominion over them. It contained my sentiments then ; you will see how far they accord with my sentiments now. Time has more and more confirmed me in them all. The present circumstances fix them deeper in my mind.

I voted last session, if a particular vote could be distinguished, in unanimity, for an establishment of the Church of England conjointly with the establishment, which was made some years before by Act of Parliament, of the Roman Catholic, in the French conquered country of Canada. At the time of making this English ecclesiastical establishment, we did not think it necessary for its safety to destroy the former Gallican Church settlement. In our first Act we settled a government altogether monarchical, or nearly so. In that system the Canadian Catholics were far from being deprived of the advantages or distinctions, of any kind, which they enjoyed under their former monarchy. It is true that some people, and amongst them one eminent divine, predicted at that time that by this step we

should lose our dominions in America. He foretold
that the Pope would send his indulgences thither;
that the Canadians would fall in with France,
would declare independence, and draw or force
our colonies into the same design. The independence happened according to his prediction; but
in directly the reverse order. All our English Protestant colonies revolted. They joined themselves
to France; and it so happened that Popish Canada
was the only place which preserved its fidelity; the
only place in which France got no footing; the only
peopled colony which now remains to Great Britain.
Vain are all the prognostics taken from ideas and
passions which survive the state of things which
gave rise to them. When last year we gave a
popular representation to the same Canada, by the
choice of the landholders and an aristocratic representation, at the choice of the Crown, neither was the
choice of the Crown nor the election of the landholders limited by a consideration of religion. We
had no dread for the Protestant Church, which we
settled there, because we permitted the French
Catholics, in the utmost latitude of the description,
to be free subjects. They are good subjects, I have
no doubt; but I will not allow that any French
Canadian Catholics are better men or better citizens
than the Irish of the same communion. Passing
from the extremity of the West to the extremity
almost of the East, I have been many years (now

entering into the twelfth) employed in supporting the
rights, privileges, laws, and immunities of a very
remote people.   I have not as yet been able to
finish my task.   I have struggled through much dis-
couragement and much opposition, much obloquy,
much calumny, for a people with whom I have no
tie but the common bond of mankind.   In this I
have not been left alone.   We did not fly from our
undertaking because the people are Mahometans or
Pagans, and that a great majority of the Christians
amongst them are Papists.   Some gentlemen in
Ireland, I dare say, have good reasons for what they
may do, which do not occur to me.   I do not
presume to condemn them ; but, thinking and acting
as I have done towards these remote nations, I should
not know how to show my face, here or in Ireland, if
I should say that all the Pagans, all the Mussulmen,
and even all the Papists (since they must form the
highest stage in the climax of evil) are worthy of a
liberal and honourable condition, except those of one
of the descriptions, which forms the majority of the
inhabitants of the country in which you and I were
born.   If such are the Catholics of Ireland, ill-
natured and unjust people, from our own data, may
be inclined not to think better of the Protestants of
a soil which is supposed to infuse into its sects a kind
of venom unknown in other places.

You hated the old system as early as I did.
Your first juvenile lance was broken against that

giant. I think you were even the first who attacked the grim phantom. You have an exceeding good understanding, very good humour, and the best heart in the world. The dictates of that temper and that heart, as well as the policy pointed out by that understanding, led you to abhor the old code. You abhorred it, as I did, for its vicious perfection. For I must do it justice : it was a complete system, full of coherence and consistency ; well digested and well composed in all its parts. It was a machine of wise and elaborate contrivance, and as well fitted for the oppression, impoverishment, and degradation of a people, and the debasement in them of human nature itself, as ever proceeded from the perverted ingenuity of man. It is a thing humiliating enough, that we are doubtful of the effect of the medicines we compound. We are sure of our poisons. My opinion ever was (in which I heartily agreed with those that admired the old code) that it was so constructed that if there was once a breach in any essential part of it, the ruin of the whole, or nearly of the whole, was at some time or other a certainty. For that reason I honour, and shall for ever honour and love you, and those who first caused it to stagger, crack, and gape. Others may finish ; the beginners have the glory ; and, take what part you please at this hour (I think you will take the best), your first services will never be forgotten by a grateful country.

Adieu! Present my best regards to those I know ; and as many as I know in our country, I honour. There never was so much ability, or, I believe, virtue in it. They have a task worthy of both. I doubt not they will perform it, for the stability of the Church and State, and for the union and the separation of the people : for the union of the honest and peaceable of all sects—for their separation from all that is ill-intentioned and seditious in any of them.

BEACONSFIELD,
January 3, 1792.

PRINTED BY BALLANTYNE, HANSON AND CO.
LONDON AND EDINBURGH

www.ingramcontent.com/pod-product-compliance
Lightning Source LLC
Chambersburg PA
CBHW030339270326
41926CB00009B/890